Reykjavik

Text: James Proctor and Lance Price
Principal Photographer: Britta Jaschinski
Managing Editor: Clare Peel
Series Editor: Tony Halliday

D1335167

Berlitz® POCKET GUIDE

Reykjavík

First Edition 2005

PHOTOGRAPHY
By Britta Jaschinski except: 3 (centre), 15, 17, 20, 69, 76, 77, 79, 81, 90 Lance Price/Apa; 11, 71, 72 Icelandic Tourist Board/Photo: Dieter Schweizer; 85, 102 Icelandic Tourist Board/Photo: Randall Hyman; 64 Hans Klüche; 60 Icelandic Tourist Board; 74 Icelandic Tourist Board/Photo: Thierry des Ouches; 8 Visit Reykjavík; 3 (bottom right) Icelandic Tourist Board/www.bluelagoon.is.
Cover photograph: Bo Zaunders/Corbis

CONTACTING THE EDITORS
Every effort has been made to provide accurate information in this publication, but changes are inevitable. The publisher cannot be responsible for any resulting loss, inconvenience or injury. We would appreciate it if readers would call our attention to any errors or outdated information by contacting Berlitz Publishing, PO Box 7910, London SE1 1WE, England.
Fax: (44) 20 7403 0290;
e-mail: berlitz@apaguide.co.uk
www.berlitzpublishing.com

➤ Reykjavík's art galleries include the Ásmundur Sveinsson Sculpture Museum (page 52)

◄ Take in breathtaking views of Reykjavík from the Perlan hilltop museum and restaurant complex (page 48)

The Hallgrímskirkja (page 28), with its sweeping spire, dominates the city's skyline ▼

TOP TEN ATTRACTIONS

Geysir and Gullfoss (pages 62–5) make a popular day out from Reykjavík

Tjörnin (page 38), the city-centre lake, is teeming with birdlife during the summer months

Many people come to the Icelandic capital for its hip nightlife (page 83)

See Iceland's history, including the Sagas, at the Culture House (page 32)

Jón Gunnar Árnason designed the stainless-steel Sólfar suncraft (page 45)

Take a boat trip from Reykjavík harbour (page 40) to spot whales

The naturally heated waters of the Blue Lagoon (page 65) are renowned for their therapeutic effects

CONTENTS

Fact Sheets

INTRODUCTION

Few places on earth can match the raw and intense beauty of Reykjavík. Surrounded by majestic snow-capped mountains and immense lavafields, the world's most northerly capital is a place of dramatic contrasts. A stroll through the streets of the Icelandic capitals not only conjures up picturesque houses painted a mêlée of reds, yellows and greens but it also provides a glimpse of the wild nature that surrounds this city: the steely grey waters of the North Atlantic surging into countless bays and inlets, the brilliant white light of the northern sky and the city-centre lake, Tjörnin, teeming with birdlife. Indeed, millions of birds flock to Iceland's cliff tops and coastal meadows to nest during the bright summer months, while offshore, whales, dolphins and seals are abundant in some of the cleanest waters on earth. A short drive from Reykjavík will bring you to vast ice fields, bubbling mud pools, colossal waterfalls and hot springs. However, should you choose to stay in the city you'll be rewarded with an extensive bar and restaurant scene and some buzzing nightlife, too. Reykjavík also boasts a rich cultural scene – there's an impressive array of museums and galleries as well as regularly changing exhibitions of local art across the city.

Underground Drama
In geological terms, Iceland is a mere babe, composed of some of the youngest rocks on earth and still being formed. Over the centuries,

During the darkest months of the year there are only four hours of daylight in Reykjavík, whilst conversely during the height of summer the sun is above the horizon for 21 hours.

View over the city rooftops

The Perlan provides Reykjavík with hot water and heating

eruptions have spewed vast fields of lava across the island's surface and projected choking clouds of ash high into the air, blocking out the sunlight and blighting crops. Recent eruptions have been less destructive, but no less spectacular, than earlier ones; every day there are thousands of minor earthquakes and small shocks, most of which are only detectable by seismologists. The presence of so much natural energy just below ground makes it possible not just to see the awesome power of nature, but to feel, hear and smell it. The limitless reserves of geothermal energy that have produced such a varied terrain also supply heat and power to Iceland's homes, and the 'rotten egg' smell of sulphur is unmistakable. Dams across fast-flowing glacial rivers provide the nation with more than enough hydroelectrically generated power to meet its needs.

The abundant hot water not only heats homes and offices, in winter it is piped under pavements in the centre of Reykjavík to melt away the snow and ice. And year round it contributes to the social life of the Icelanders, filling outdoor swimming pools, where people meet to take a little exercise or just to chat in the hot tubs and steam rooms.

Pollution-Free Land

For Reykjavíkers, keeping their city clean and pollution-free is a top priority. It's with justifiable pride that they boast that the water from any stream or non-glacial river in the country is drinkable, due in no small part to the absence of heavy industry. The air in Reykjavík is bitingly clean and among the cleanest you'll find anywhere in Europe. You won't see rubbish tipped at the wayside here, nor will you encounter widespread burning of fossil fuels. Recently, the government has attempted to attract new heavy industry such as aluminium smelting, which needs high amounts of energy; however, the environmental impact of the new dams that would be required have roused huge controversy.

High Standard of Living

Reykjavík enjoys one of the highest standards of living of any city in the world. A European nation, Iceland remains outside the European Union mainly to protect its economically vital fishing grounds. It has strong social institutions and a well-funded welfare system. Few Icelanders are conspicuously rich, but there's little urban poverty, and health care and education facilities throughout the country are highly developed. Reykjavík remains, though, the richest and most-sought after place to live in the country.

Smoky Bay's Steamy Power

The name Reykjavík, meaning 'smoky bay', was coined by one of the early settlers who mistook the steam rising from the ground for smoke. Inevitably the arrival of Man brought pollution in its wake, especially with the burning of fossil fuels. As the city expanded massively in the 20th century, so did the threat from polluted air. The decision, taken in the 1960s, to convert the city to environmentally friendly power sources cut carbon dioxide emissions from the heating system alone from 270,000 tonnes a year to virtually zero. Today, the geothermally heated water that gave the city its name is used to heat its buildings and is even piped beneath the main streets in winter to prevent icing. Reykjavík is arguably the world's greenest capital city.

Reykjavíkers make the most of the many benefits of their extraordinary environment, spending as much time as possible outdoors, weather-permitting. Walking, climbing and horseriding are popular pursuits, and, as the importance of tourism has grown, so too has the number of companies offering snowmobiling on the glaciers, hiking adventures in the interior and whale-watching off the coast.

Small but Perfectly Formed

In European terms Reykjavík is a small and compact place – its population is barely 110,000. Although Iceland is equal in size to England and has plenty of undeveloped land, roughly three out of every five Icelanders live in and around the capital. The people of this Nordic capital have a powerful respect for nature and know they can never expect to control it or have it all to themselves.

Friendly locals

Dominated by brightly painted buildings and a massive central church, Reykjavík is a lively place. Here, a modern, cosmopolitan city has evolved beneath snow-capped mountains. The population may be small, but it's very clear from the cafes, restaurants and nightclubs that this is a place where people know how to have a good time. However, the scene starts late, and the often high prices for alcohol and a decent meal force many locals to get their eating and a fair bit of their drinking done at home before they venture out.

Long Days of Summer
The weather in Reykjavík is extremely changeable. Winters are cold and dark, with a moderate amount of snowfall. Light relief is provided

The glorious midnight sun

at night by the spectral glow of the northern lights *(aurora borealis)*. It's only in summer, when the temperatures rise and the long days are often bright and sunny, that Reykjavík can really be seen in its true colours – flowers are in full bloom, the air is alive with birdsong, and the long summer nights barely show any sign of darkness. Remember that Reykjavík is at its most lively and animated between May and September – definitely the best time to visit. Similarly, the bus companies don't run a full service until late June, something to bear in mind if you're planning a couple of trips out of the capital by bus. Air schedules tend not to show any great difference between winter and summer.

Hot Springs and Outdoor Baths
Since the late 1970s Iceland's only major road, a vast circular route around the coast, has linked village to town, countryside to capital. Most communities are found on or near the ring road, a short distance from the sea, where the land is at its flattest and most fertile. This narrow coastal plain, the only truly habitable part of the country, makes up just one-fifth of Iceland's total area.

Fortunately, much of the most impressive scenery is easily accessible from Reykjavík. A worthwhile tour around the Golden Circle takes in the original Geysir, which gave its name to all geysers around the world, the Gullfoss waterfall and the Þingvellir Viking parliament site. The tour is easily covered from Reykjavík. So too is the best outdoor bath on the planet, the Blue Lagoon. The Westman Islands, a short plane or ferry ride from the capital, are equally demanding of your attention, while a trip to one of Iceland's glaciers is also a distinct possibility.

Despite the rigours of its landscape, Reykjavík – and indeed the rest of Iceland – is a very welcoming place. Its people aren't given to great outward shows of emotion but they are intensely proud of their city and will offer an embrace that is as sincere as it is warm to the visitor who's willing to respect their capital's unique location on the very edge of the Arctic.

Taking a break in Lækjartorg

A BRIEF HISTORY

While elsewhere in Europe, civilisations, empires and dynasties came and went, Iceland remained uninhabited and undiscovered. It wasn't until the 8th century AD that Irish monks became the first people known to have set foot on the island, relishing its solitude. They left no physical trace behind either, nor, being all men, any new generation. Within just 100 years, however, the peace they had enjoyed was no longer: the Vikings were coming. Much of Iceland's history was chronicled within a few hundred years of the events happening. The *Landnámabók* (Book of Settlements), written in the 12th century, describes in detail the first permanent inhabitants. The sagas, dramatic tales of early Iceland penned 100 years later, give a lot more colour to the story in the form of fiction.

The Founding of Reykjavík

The country's first permanent settlers were Norwegians escaping political persecution and economic hardship at home. They found Iceland quite by accident, having already colonised parts of both Scotland and the Faroe Islands. The official 'First Settler' was Ingólfur Arnarson, who enjoyed his first winter so much that he went to fetch his extended family and friends to come and join him. They brought with them farm animals, paganism and Irish slaves, some of whom would cause

> Although many Icelanders can trace their families back to the early settlers, family names do not exist. Instead, children absorb their father's first name into their own. A man named Eiríkur Gúðbrandsson might, for example, have a son named Leifur Eiríksson and a daughter named Þórdís Eiríksdóttir.

Statue of Ingólfur Arnason, the first settler on Iceland

mutiny and kill their owners. However, there was no indigenous population for the colonisers to evict or butcher, and the biggest threat they faced was from the elements.

Having spent three years roaming Iceland's southern coast, Ingólfur eventually settled in 874 in the bay that is now home to the capital, Reykjavík (*vík* means 'bay'). It was here that his high seat pillars – a potent symbol of Viking chieftainship – were finally washed up after being tossed overboard from Ingólfur's boat when he first approached Icelandic shores three or four years earlier. He named the location *reykjavík*, or smoky bay, after the plumes of steam that he saw issuing from nearby hotsprings.

These first Icelanders established farms in the rather more hospitable parts of the country. Some basic laws were already in place: a man could claim as much land as he could light bonfires around in one day, as long as each one could be seen from the others; and women could have as much land as a heifer could walk around in a day. Inevitably, however, disputes broke out, which the local chieftains had to resolve. When they failed, there could be bloody battles. Population growth was slow due to the severe climatic conditions and constant disease; indeed by 1786, the population of Reykjavík town barely numbered 176 souls.

The First Parliament

In AD 930 the chieftains got together and agreed on a relatively democratic system of government. A Commonwealth was established, with a national assembly or Alþingi meeting for two weeks every summer at a flat plain southeast of Reykjavík, Þingvellir, which could be reached relatively easily from all parts of the country. Here, new laws would be agreed and infringements of old laws settled by a system of regional courts. The worst punishment was to be declared an outlaw and banished from the country.

The system wasn't perfect, and there were still some bloody battles – these were, after all, the descendants of Vikings, who valued courage and honour above all else. Nonetheless this period is now considered to have been a Golden Age, the Saga Age, full of great heroes and wise men.

Viking armour

From Pagans to Christians

Soon, however, things were to change dramatically. Christianity had spread to northern Europe, and the zealous, if bloodthirsty, King Ólafur Tryggvason of Norway wanted Iceland for the new religion too. When his missionaries encountered resistance in the late 10th century, he was all for butchering the entire population until the Icelandic chieftain Gizur the White promised to have another go by more peaceful means. Fortunately, the lawspeaker, who presided over the Alþingi, was at that time the widely respected Þorgeir. He persuaded both sides to agree to accept his decision in advance and then went off to meditate. He came back and announced that Iceland would become Christian, although pagans could continue to practise their beliefs in private.

Bishoprics, monasteries and schools quickly followed, and books were soon being written for the first time. As a sign of their independence the writers chose to do their work in Icelandic, not Latin. There were so few foreign influences in the centuries to come that the language they used is almost identical to the Icelandic that is spoken today.

The Sagas

Between the 12th and 15th centuries some of the great stories the Icelanders had previously passed on from generation to generation were written down. Collectively known as *The Sagas* (literally 'things told'), they are some of the most dramatic and compelling tales in world literature. Scholars argue about how accurate they are, but for good old-fashioned story telling they are unbeatable. Families are torn apart by feuds, knights ride off to battle in shining armour, saints are saintly, the wicked are truly wicked, and mythical dragons and dwarves stalk the land. They are written in an unemotional style that makes the brutal fates of many of their characters even more shocking. The manuscripts were collected for posterity by Árni Magnússon (1663–1730) and taken off to Copenhagen for safety, but most were then lost in a terrible fire. Árni himself braved the flames to rescue some of them. The surviving Sagas weren't returned to Iceland until long after Independence. Perhaps wary of their troubled history, the authorities in Reykjavík keep them under lock and key, although some are put on display at the Culture House.

All was not well in the country, however, and Iceland was about to enter its Dark Age. The Hekla volcano southeast of Reykjavík erupted in 1104, burying nearby farms; over-grazing and soil erosion from excessive tree-felling further reduced the amount of viable land. At the same time the Church became greedy and, by imposing tithes, it split the formerly egalitarian society. Some chiefs, who were given church lands or made into senior clergy, found themselves increasingly rich and powerful. Before long the most important families started fighting for supremacy. The Alþingi, which had relied on people voluntarily accepting its authority, was now powerless to respond.

Illustration from the Edda Manuscript, part of the Sagas

Civil War and Black Death

Soon the country was in a state of civil war, which was ended only when Norway took sovereignty to help to maintain order in 1262. Iceland kept many of its old laws, but 700 years of foreign domination had begun.

Revolts and skirmishes continued, while nature also took its toll. Harsh winters destroyed farm animals and crops, yet more eruptions covered parts of the country in ash, and the Black Death arrived in Iceland, laying waste to half the population.

Those Icelanders still living were too busy struggling to survive to notice that Denmark had taken over the Norwegian throne and was therefore their new master. But the Danes took little interest in their new acquisition, despite it possessing something the rest of Europe suddenly wanted: cod. Fishing brought new wealth to coastal landowners, but it brought new trouble, too.

English and German adventurers started appearing offshore, fighting among themselves, indulging in piracy and trying to control the trade in dried cod. The English got the upper hand, and this became known as the English Century. The Danes eventually realised that they were losing out financially. When Denmark tried to ban the English from the country, the latter killed the governor and started bringing in their canons. By 1532, however, the tide had turned, and the English leader was killed in renewed fighting with Germany. From then on England let the Danes and Germans fight among themselves and turned their attentions elsewhere.

The Reformation

The Church was still a dominant force in the early 16th century, and when Scandinavia turned Lutheran in the 1530s it was inevitable that Iceland would soon follow suit. By the middle of the century the Protestant Reformation had been well and truly imposed on an unwilling population.

By this time, Denmark was gaining increased political authority over Iceland, and eventually complete control of the country was passed to Copenhagen. From

> **Jón Sigurðsson (1811–69) is remembered in Reykjavík by a statue in Austurvöllur for his role in campaigning for independence from Denmark. He died without seeing his dream realised, but his birthday (17 June) is now celebrated as Icelandic National Day.**

Reykjavík in the early 19th century

1602 all of Iceland's trade had to pass by law through a small group of Danish companies, a move that effectively bankrupted the country. Smallpox then wiped out almost a third of the impoverished population, and, just when it seemed as if matters could not get any worse, thousands more citizens were killed in 1783–4 by massive eruptions that poisoned almost the entire country and caused widespread famine. Denmark considered evacuating the whole surviving population, but decided instead to relax the trading laws a little and give the country a chance to recover.

As it did so, educated Icelanders looked to continental Europe and saw democracy stirring in once-powerful monarchies. Jónas Hallgrímsson, a poet, and Jón Sigurðsson, a historian, started a fledgling independence movement. By 1843 they succeeded in getting the Alþingi, suspended since 1800, revived as a consultative assembly. A decade later trade was freed up completely. Slowly, prosperity started to return.

Fishing is still big business

In 1874 Denmark, which was now a constitutional monarchy, returned complete legislative powers to the Alþingi. The tithe system was abolished, schooling became compulsory, and the fishing industry was allowed to grow and prosper. By 1900 Iceland had its own political parties. In 1904 it was granted Home Rule and in 1918 gained independence in return for keeping the Danish king as monarch.

War and Peace

Iceland, now trading with both England and Germany, stayed neutral in World War I, although its growing economy was hit by the Great Depression of the 1930s. During World War II control of the North Atlantic was a key strategic objective, and first Britain, then the US, landed forces in Iceland and occupied Reykjavík. Denmark was invaded by Germany, and its ties to Iceland were finally cut when full independence was declared on 17 June 1944. Reykjavík now became the capital of a sovereign country and inherited all the trappings of state including a president, fully fledged parliament and a seat at the United Nations (UN).

Reykjavík's strategic location made the new government feel nervous, as the Cold War gripped the western world. In response it joined the UN and then NATO, a controversial decision that provoked riots in Reykjavík during which the parliament was attacked and police stormed the protestors with tear gas – one of the rare outbreaks of violence in Iceland.

When Iceland next went to war, however, it was with a fellow NATO country, Britain. Fortunately nobody was killed, and the so-called Cod Wars, which came and went for 30 years after 1952, were no more than a bit of naval muscle flexing. Britain objected to successive extensions to Iceland's territorial waters and sent patrol boats to protect its trawlers. In 1975 it ordered its frigates to ram Icelandic coastguard ships, which had been cutting the cables of British trawlers. Eventually, in 1985, Reykjavík got its way, and 325-km (200-mile) limits became the norm worldwide.

Although the European Union's stringent fisheries policy has deterred Reykjavík from joining that group, since the last quarter of the 20th century the country has been increasingly outward looking, attracting foreign businesses and visitors. In 1986 the world's media descended on Reykjavík for a nuclear summit between presidents Reagan and Gorbachev,

Reykjavík's Government House

which was famously held at the Höfði house and raised the country's profile worldwide.

Although international protests forced Iceland to ban commercial whaling in 1989, the Reykjavík government – highly controversially – gave permission for scientific whaling to recommence in August 2003 amid ongoing concern over whale stocks beyond the country's borders. A limited number of minke whales are now caught by whaling vessles berthed in Reykjavík harbour for scientific research purposes, albeit within the jurisdiction of the International Whaling Commission, which Reykjavík rejoined in late 2002 *(see also page 43)*. In addition to the pros and cons of whaling, the current dilemmas facing all Icelanders, not only those in Reykjavík, is how best to protect the natural beauty of their country and yet allow its economy to keep pace with other European nations.

Looking to the future

Iceland remains dependent on fishing, but new developments, such as using natural energy to grow hothouse crops, for example in Hveragerdi outside Reykjavík, show its willingness to diversify. All in all, Reykjavík is a forward-thinking capital city that is happy to co-operate with the world community, yet is reluctant to be dictated to by it.

Historical Landmarks

874 Reykjavík is founded by the Viking Ingólfur Arnarson and his family.

930 Creation of the Alþingi parliament southeast of Reykjavík.

1000 Christianity is adopted as Iceland's official religion.

13th and 14th centuries Feuding between Norway and Denmark over the ruling of Iceland. Reykjavík loses power to Copenhagen.

1389 Huge eruption of Mt Hekla devastates farming land around Reykjavík. Black Death decimates the town.

1662–1854 Reykjavík traders hit by Danish trade monopoly.

1783 Eruption of Laki volcano poisons the land, leading to famine in Reykjavík.

1800 Danish King abolishes the Alþingi; it is reinstated in 1843.

1904 Iceland is granted limited home rule. Reykjavík becomes the capital.

1918 Iceland made a sovereign state under the Act of Union with Denmark. Danish king is head of state.

1940 British forces arrive in Reykjavík to occupy Iceland.

1944 Independence from Denmark declared on 17 June.

1947 Last American soldiers leave Keflavík air base.

1948 US Marshall aid pours in to Iceland. Money used to build a power station and fertiliser plant near Reykjavík.

1949 Iceland becomes a founding member of NATO provoking riots in Reykjavík. Police retaliate with tear gas.

1951 Keflavík air base reestablished; arrival of 5000 American troops.

1952–76 Cod Wars (1952, 1958, 1972, 1975) with the UK.

1963 Surtsey island created by an underwater volcanic eruption.

1968 Iceland changes over to driving on the right.

1973 Volcanic eruption on Heimaey island.

1986 Reykjavík summit between presidents Reagan and Gorbachev.

1994 Iceland enters the European Economic Area.

2000 Mt Hekla eruption in February; earthquakes in June. Reykjavík becomes a European City of Culture.

2002 Iceland rejoins the International Whaling Commission.

2003 Iceland begins scientific whaling after 14 years.

2004 Eruptions of volcanoes on Vatnajökull.

WHERE TO GO

Reykjavík may not be the world's largest or most vibrant capital city – many average sized towns in Europe or the US are bigger – but it does contain a surprisingly wide range of sights and activities for the visitor. You will quickly get the sense that Icelanders are immensely proud of their country and of Reykjavík in particular. They love living here and very much want visitors to enjoy what the city has to offer. Given its size, a huge amount of time and effort has gone into bringing Reykjavík's museums, galleries, churches and public buildings, parks and sports facilities up to international standards.

> If Reykjavík feels a long way from anywhere, it's not surprising given that it really is at the edge of the world. Situated at 64.08ºN it is the world's most northerly capital city. And at 21.55ºW, it is Europe's most westerly.

For those on a relatively short visit, it's possible to see most of the principal city sights in a full day, leaving time to explore the major attractions that are just a short journey from the capital – the Golden Circle, the Blue Lagoon or the Westman Islands, for example. Those who are fortunate enough to be able to stay a little longer, however, will find no shortage of things to keep them occupied and entertained in Reykjavík for several days at least.

It doesn't take long to spot what makes Reykjavík so very different from most other capital cities. There are virtually no high-rise buildings, absolutely no skyscrapers, and the use of corrugated iron and timber in many of the buildings makes them look almost temporary. In fact, the construction materials

The Ásmundursafn (Asmundur Sveinsson Sculpture Museum)

and layout of the city are very practical and, like everything else in Iceland, are designed with the elements in mind.

Half the population of Iceland live in the country's capital, where they enjoy fresh air and a magnificent location between a bay and the mountains and glaciers of the interior. Apart from a few major roads around the edge of town, the streets are narrow and sometimes steep. Reykjavík is a delight, not just for what it has but for what it doesn't have: traffic jams, pollution, jostling crowds, busy commuters packing the buses and streets. After just a short amount of time, you come to realise that Reykjavík manages to have all the best aspects of a city – the shops, restaurants, bars and museums – with few of the inconveniences that can make other capitals such hard work. And its manageable size means that almost everything you'll want to see is either within walking distance or a short bus or taxi ride away.

The heart of the city: Tjörnin lake

Visitors to Reykjavík vary dramatically, from those in search of a quick clubbing weekend, to those on a short stopover en route to North America, to others who are here as part of a much longer exploration of Iceland as a whole, often involving camping, hiking or other outdoor pursuits. Either way, the magnificent Hallgrímskirkja church should number among

Contemporary City Hall

your top sights, as should the City Hall, the enchanting Tjörnin lake and the historic government buildings. The Culture House lives up to its name with a terrific overview of Icelandic culture and the reopening of the National Museum has been a long awaited addition to the city's attractions.

Culturally, Iceland may seem in some ways very foreign indeed to some visitors, but fortunately the country and its traditions are very accessible. The tourist industry in Iceland works almost exclusively in English, so there's little need to try to get to grips with the potentially intimidating intricacies of the Icelandic language. Getting around is easy: in Reykjavík the public transport system is clean and reliable, although you probably won't always need it, as many of the central sights can be explored comfortably on foot.

CENTRAL REYKJAVÍK

As you fly into Reykjavík, the enormous church at the centre of the city looks like some kind of rocket ship about to take to the sky itself. Indeed, on the drive in from the airport at Keflavík across the wide expanse of lava fields, the massive bulk of Hallgrímskirkja is, if anything, even more evident.

Taking in the views from Hallgrímskirkja's tower

The church is so enormous and its futuristic lines so distinctive that the building not only dominates the skyline, it also seems to reduce everything else to insignificance. The eye is constantly drawn back to it, regardless of where you find yourself in the city, and it can be an invaluable landmark in terms of getting one's bearings.

The church is the most obvious place to begin a city tour, and unless you are staying in one of the hotels nearby you will almost certainly approach it up Skólavörðustígur. Getting up the street can feel more like a climb than a walk, but as you head for Hallgrímskirkja, don't rush. Take time to look in the windows of the numerous little art galleries that have sprung up here in recent years. The standard of the work is consistently high and shows just how much artistic talent such a small country is capable of producing.

Hallgrímskirkja

What breath you have left after the climb will be taken away by the sight of **Hallgrímskirkja** (off Bergþórugata; open daily May–Sept 9am–6pm, Oct– Apr 10am–4pm; free) from right up close. The curves and the symmetry are even more impressive from here. Check the time on the clock face, too. It may well be wrong – the strong winds that blow across Reykjavík make keeping the clock accurate a never-ending battle. Designed by Guðjón Samúelsson, and having been in almost constant construction since the end of World War II, the church is a monument not only to Christ but also to Reykjavík's belief that being small need not limit its ambitions. The steeple is 73m (240ft) high and has a viewing platform (open daily 9am–5pm, May–Sept until 6pm; admission charge), which is accessed by a lift from just inside the door. From here you can enjoy magnificent views not only of the city but also of the surrounding mountains – something that gives a good sense of a community living comfortably alongside an often hostile environment. (Just to amplify the point, you may get a blast of those strong winds bringing cold air straight in from the snow-covered peaks.)

The interior of the church itself is very bare, as befits its Lutheran status, and there is not much to see except the magnificent organ, which is 15m (50ft) high and has more than 5,000 pipes.

Leifur Eiríksson's statue stands in front of Hallgrímskirkja

Just outside the church is a **statue of Leifur Eiríksson**, Iceland's greatest adventurer, who reached America long before Christopher Columbus. The statue, by A. Stirling Calder, was a gift from the US government to mark the Icelandic parliament's 1,000th anniversary in 1930. The explorer is looking in the direction of America, still waiting for the full recognition his bravery really deserves.

On 11 July almost every museum in Reykjavík participates in Icelandic Museum Day, with special events, exhibitions and special guest appearances held. The tourist office *(see page 129)* will have full details of the latest attractions.

Einar Jónsson Museum

And, on the subject of sculpture, nearby is a museum dedicated to Einar Jónsson (1874–1954), one of Iceland's greatest modern exponents of that art: the **Safn Einars Jónssonar** (Einar Jónsson Museum; Njarðargata; open June–mid-Sept Tues–Sun 2–5pm, mid-Sept–May Sat, Sun 2–5pm; admission charge). The entrance to the museum is on Freyjugata, on the opposite side of the building from the church. Jónsson had the house constructed himself and lived here as a virtual recluse towards the end of his life. As a result, many people detect a real feeling of isolation in the 100 or so pieces exhibited in the building and the adjoining garden, where more of his sculptures stand. Most of the works are decidedly dark and sombre in character.

ASÍ and Ásgrímur Jónsson Collection

If you have an appetite for more art, continue down Freyjugata to No. 41, to the ASÍ (open all year Tues–Sun 2–6pm; free), a gallery run by the Icelandic Labour Unions and showcasing a mixture of works by both renowned Icelandic painters and visiting exhibitors. Rather more dramatic is the **Ásgrímssafn** (Ásgrímur Jónsson Collection; Bergstaðastræti 74; open June–Aug Tues–Sun 1.30–4pm; admission charge), the former home of one of Iceland's most celebrated painters. One room on the ground floor is left just as it was when Jónsson lived here, with his beloved piano taking centre stage, while upstairs there are examples of his often colourful and emotional works of art. His love of the environment and Iceland's sometimes violent history shines through in every one.

Laugavegur

At the bottom of Skólavördustígur is Reykjavík's main shopping street, **Laugavegur**. The name translates literally as 'Hot Spring Road', and it means what it says – it was once the path taken by townspeople who were going to do their laundry in the hot pools in Laugardalur *(see page 53)*. Today, thanks to the city's unique geothermal heating system, the same source is used to help to keep the roads ice-free in winter, using underground water piped up from the springs. Laugavegur is the nearest thing Iceland's capital has to a boulevard or avenue and it is home to a mixture of international shops, local stores of all kinds and a wide selection of cafes, bars, restaurants and hotels. It may not be Oxford Street or Fifth Avenue but it's still something of a sight in itself. The street is long, straight and narrow and crying out for pedestrianisation, but window shopping and people-watching along here provide as good an

Shopping on Reykjavík's main commercial thoroughfare: Laugavegur

Hip fashions on Laugavegur

insight as any into modern Icelandic life. High fashion rubs shoulders with the highly practical, and local crafts hold their own alongside consumer goods from all over the world. One look at the price tags may convince you that Iceland is indeed as expensive as everybody says it is, although there are some bargains to be found *(see page 86)*. The best of the shops are at the western end of the street, where they extend into Bankastræti and then along Lækjargata and into the narrower little roads between the harbour and the City Hall.

The Culture House

Just a short distance from all the commercial outlets is one of Reykjavík's most impressive museums, the **Þjódmenningarhusið** (Culture House; Hverfisgata 15; open daily 11am– 5pm; admission charge). This fine listed building was opened in 1909 and intended principally to house the National Library. For a time it also included the National Museum and National History Museum, but these now have buildings of their own. The Culture House is now a fairly academic place, although many of its exhibitions are colourful as well as educational. A fascinating series of exhibits on Icelandic history takes you right back to the first settlers. It is well illustrated and has plenty of vivid depictions of early life in Iceland to keep adults and children alike informed and entertained. You can see the story of the Vikings and their travels around the North Atlantic, with models of the kinds of ships they used, their weapons and armour.

The Culture House also contains a good collection of memorabilia from the lengthy struggle for independence in the 19th and 20th centuries along with portraits of some of the key political figures of the period. In 2004 a new exhibition was opened to celebrate the centenary of Home Rule for Iceland. You can see the decrees that recognised the principle of parliamentary government and the new Icelandic coat of arms, a white gyrfalcon on a blue background.

The most valuable exhibits, and in many ways the most interesting, are the collection of manuscripts dating from the 12th and 13th centuries, including some of the first documents composed in Icelandic. You can see the world-famous **Sagas** as they were originally written. Their survival is largely thanks to the efforts of Árni Magnússon (1663–1730), who saw the damage the climate was doing to the old texts and collected as many as he could and whisked them

The Culture House is home to the Sagas

away to Copenhagen for safe keeping. Tragically, many were then lost in the Great Fire that swept through the Danish capital in 1728. Those that remained were a source of constant dispute beteen the Danes and the Icelanders until the last of them was finally returned at the end of the 20th century. They remain a potent symbol of Icelandic nationhood, and television screens alongside the exhibits still show the original news reports of their repatriation.

In the loft of the building is an experience for real lovers of museums for their own sakes. The display is in effect a recreation of an exhibition that was held here from 1908 to 1950 and is designed to show how the role, nature and origins of museums have changed over the years. The effect is deliberately very cramped and often confusing, but it does show what museum-goers used to have to put up with in the first half of the last century.

The Living Art Museum

A few streets away is a venue that prides itself on being everything that the Culture House isn't, in terms of its modernity. The **Nýlistasafnið** (Living Art Museum, Vatnsstígur 3; open all year Tues–Sun 2–5pm; admission charge), or LAM, as it is known, is a non-profit-making gallery committed to providing

---

Reykjavík Tourist Card

Before you start exploring the capital, consider investing in a Reykjavík Tourist Card. It can be purchased from the tourist office, bus terminals, museums, the City Hall Information Desk and many hotels for a cost of 1,200 lkr for 24 hours, 1,700 lkr for 48 hours and 2,200 lsk for 72 hours. The card gives access to 10 museums and galleries, the Family Park and Zoo and all seven of the city's swimming pools. It also entitles the holder to free travel on the city buses.

a forum for the most innovative and cutting-edge art in the country. Since it was founded in 1978 it has been building up an impressive permanent collection, helped by the fact that all artists who join the association have to donate an example of their work. In addition there are eight to ten larger exhibitions a year as well as performance art, readings and concerts.

Cafe on Bankastræti

Government District

At the western end of Laugavegur, after it changes its name to Bankastræti, is the district where most of Iceland's government buildings are to be found. None is particularly grand or ostentatious, as befits a country that has never had any imperial ambitions of its own. And very much to its credit the Icelandic government has never felt the need to build great monuments to its own importance.

Stjónarráðið (Government House), an isolated, low white building at the western end of Bankastræti, is closed to the public. It is a modest-looking affair but is notable nonetheless for being one of the oldest surviving houses in the country (it dates from 1761). It was originally built as a prison but it now houses the office of the prime minister, although he doesn't live there.

On the opposite side of the street, there is an imposing **statue** of Iceland's first settler, Ingólfur Arnarson, looking out over the Atlantic. Behind him is the **Þjóðleikhúsið** (National Theatre Building), which is only open to the public during performances. Along the road towards the sea are several of the government ministries.

Around Austurvöller

Back in the direction of the lake is the building that houses the headquarters of the Icelandic Parliament. There are only 63 members of parliament for the whole country, and their assembly building, the attractive, grey-basalt **Alþingishúsið** (Parliament Building, Austurvöllur Square; not open to the public), dating from 1881, is almost lost among the surrounding streets. When the members of parliament are sitting, their debates are open to the public (Mon–Wed from 1.30pm, Thur from 10.30pm; free), but, of course, you would need to understand Icelandic to appreciate the finer points of their arguments.

The grey basalt Icelandic Parliament

The square in front of the parliament, **Austurvöllur**, is one of Reykjavík's most pleasant public places. It is away from the major roads and has neat lawns, well-kept flower beds and a very friendly atmosphere. Local people and tourists alike use it regularly as a place to enjoy a cup of coffee or a lunchtime sandwich. This

Picking flowers on Austurvöller

was originally the centre of Reykjavík, when the city was much smaller than it is today. Rising up above the square, almost as if it is keeping watch over the liberated people, is the statue of one of Iceland's most celebrated campaigners for independence, **Jón Sigurðsson** *(see page 18)*. Also known as *The Pride of Iceland*, the statue faces the parliament Sigurðsson campaigned for all his life.

A couple of streets away is a much larger, busier and less attractive square, **Lækjartorg**, surrounded by numerous fast-food outlets and coffee bars.

Just west of the parliament building is Reykjavík's Lutheran cathedral **Dómkirkjan** (open Mon–Fri 10am–5pm; free). Although this is the seat of the country's predominant religion, it has none of the dramatic architecture of Hallgrímskirkja, although what it lacks in size it makes up for in understated charm. It was started in 1785 and finished a decade later. Behind its rather plain façade is a quite dramatic interior with high arched windows that bathe the place in light. Unfortunately, it is now too small for most major state occasions, and most of these now take place in Hallgrímskirkja. Further west is the rather dour **Kathólska kirkjan**, or Roman

Houses clad in corrugated metal are a common sight in Reykjavík – a tradition that dates back to when all houses were made of timber. Corrugated metal is an excellent shield against the elements – vital in blustery Iceland – and allows the timber to breathe, so it is still used to cover timber houses today.

Catholic Cathedral, on Túngata. Only about one percent of the Icelandic population is Catholic, and very few other people bother to make the trek out to see this building.

Tjörnin

South of the parliament is another of the city's most pleasant outdoor locations, **Tjörnin** lake. It is a natural freshwater lake and is home to an extensive range of ducks and birds. Some of them are quite rare, and, other than in winter when it freezes over, Tjörnin is always teeming with life. Of course, the fact that there are usually children and adults happily throwing them bread may be one reason why the birds keep coming back. Noticeboards along the footpath that goes around the lake explain all about the various species, including their migration and feeding patterns.

On one edge of the lake is the **Raðhús** (Reykjavík City Hall, corner of Tjarnargata and Vonarstræti; open Mon–Fri 8am–7pm, Sat, Sun noon–6pm; free), which is accessed from the city centre side by a wooden walkway. Opened in 1992, the City Hall is a huge affair in glass and steel and is by any standards an excellent example of modern Nordic architecture. It has a cosy little cafe with free internet access, a good place to take a break from sightseeing, and a large exhibition space. On permanent display here is a huge topographical model of Iceland. If you don't have time to visit the whole of the island yourself you can at least get some idea of what you're missing right here.

The National Art Gallery and Vicinity

Alongside the lake to the east is **Listasafn Íslands** (National
Art Gallery, Fríkirkjuvegur 7; open Tues–Sun 11am–5pm;
admission charge, Wed free). This grand white building was
originally used to store blocks of ice taken from the frozen
lake to help to preserve the fish catch during the winter
months. It was not designed as an exhibition space and, compared with some of the city's galleries, is very cramped – as
a result, much of its standing collection has to be kept hidden
away in storage. Although it has only two exhibition rooms
it still manages to squeeze in examples of the work of virtually all Iceland's most famous painters, of whom the best
known internationally is probably the pop artist Erró *(see
page 78)*. Thrown in for good measure, too, are one or two
fairly minor works by great European artists including Pablo
Picasso and Edvard Munch.

Listasafn Íslands

Just south of here on the corner of Skothúsvegur are the offices of Iceland's President, and the simple but striking **Fríkirkjan** Free Lutheran Church. It's brilliant white and has a tall tower that can be useful for getting your bearings.

A couple of blocks away is the **Volcano Show** (Hellusund 6a; tel: 551 3230; open daily, July–Aug 10am–9.15pm, Sept–June 3–5.30pm; admission charge), an audio-visual experience with films in English, French and German at different times of the day. The father and son team of Ósvaldur and Vilhjálmur Knudsen have been recording volcanic activity since 1947, and the best of their images show dramatic pictures of actual eruptions, including the biggest one of recent times in 1964 that created Iceland's newest offshore island, Surtsey. The show, which lasts for about two hours, is an excellent way to learn about the way in which Iceland is being constantly reshaped by the immense power that lies just below the surface.

Ship restoration in the harbour

THE HARBOUR

Just north of the government district are the few streets that lead up to the **harbour**. This part of town is wonderfully vibrant in summer, when the many cafes, bars, restaurants and galleries in the area come to life against the backdrop of the traditional fishing industry.

At the westernmost edge of the harbour area is **Grótta Beach**, which is surprisingly quiet given how close it is to the city. This is a good spot to do a bit of bird watching or just open your nostrils and breathe in the smells of the sea, the salt and the fish.

Hafnarhúsið

Giant shipping reels

Inland a little, on Tryggvagata, is **Hafnarhúsið** (Harbour House Art Museum; open daily 11am–6pm, Thur until 7pm; admission charge, Mon free). Note that your ticket will also get you into the Kjarvalsstaðir Art Museum and the Ásmundursafn Gallery on the same day *(see page 52)*. The Harbour House is a converted warehouse that contains some extraordinary work by 20th- and 21st-century artists. It can be a little confusing to find your way around, but if you're happy to take pot luck you will certainly come across some of the best pieces by the internationally renowned Icelandic artist Erró, who donated his works to the city, as well as those by other artists from Iceland and elsewhere.

There is street art on Tryggvagata, too. High up on the wall of Tollhúsið, the old Customs House, at the junction with Pósthússtræti, there's a colourful mural, depicting the busy life of the harbour in mosaic.

City Library

The modern **Borgarbókasafn Reykjavíkur** (Reykjavík City Library, Tryggvagata 15; open all year, Mon–Fri 10am–8pm, Wed closes 7pm; Sat and Sun 1–5pm; free but charge for internet access) is tucked away on a corner in the harbour

Crates of fish are packed in ice and sent out for export

area. It's a cool and bright place, with a few books and newspapers in English and modern art displayed among the shelves. This can be a good place to get onto the internet, if the queues for the terminals aren't too long.

The Harbourfront

Reykjavík's harbour itself is still fully operational, with trawlers bringing in their catch, and crates of fish packed in ice being made ready for sale or export. Set apart from them, and looking defiant and even a little threatening are five black whaling ships, each with a red H on its funnel (the Icelandic for whale is *hvalur*). There are sometimes visiting restored or replica sailing ships along the piers, as well as cruise ships – almost 30,000 visitors a year now come to the city this way.

Today's harbour is built on reclaimed land, so you need to go a few streets back to find what used to be the old harbourfront. Here on Hafnarstræti and adjacent Aðalstræti are some of the city's most ancient buildings. Many of these have been beautifully restored and now house cafes and bars. Café Victor, Hafnarstræti 1–3, for example, was once the Fálkahúsið, where the King of Denmark kept his prize falcons. There are two carved wooden falcons on the roof to commemorate the fact.

No. 10 Aðalstræti is the oldest surviving building in Reykjavík. It dates from 1752 and once belonged to the High Sheriff of Iceland, Skúli Magnússon. When Reykjavík was little more than a town in the mid-18th century, Magnússon took it upon himself to set up local crafts and industries and bring in new skills and he is now regarded as the city's founder. Across the road outside No. 9 is a fresh-water well that is believed to have belonged to the first set-tler, Ingólfur Arnarson. It was discovered by chance during

Whales and Whaling

For many visitors, Iceland's attitude to whaling is perplexing. In almost every other way the country has a magnificent record for environmental protection and respect for nature, yet the vast majority of Icelanders support a return to commercial whaling, almost as a badge of national pride. The only thing that stops them is the fear of crippling economic sanctions from the rest of the world.

The abundance of whales off Iceland's coasts led inevitably to them being caught and killed for food. In 1948 this developed into a commercial whaling industry that continued until 1989. In less sensitive days tourists would go out of their way to watch whales being sliced up in the open air, but more recently views have hardened. Keikó, the killer whale who starred in the Hollywood film *Free Willy*, came to live in Iceland in 1998 after a campaign in the US to have him restored to his natural habitat. He improved the country's reputation as whale-friendly for a while, although he has since moved on to Norway.

In 1999 the Icelandic parliament voted to resume commercial whaling, though so far only limited scientific whaling has resumed. Icelandic boats now take to the waters to spot, rather than hunt, whales. The most common are medium-sized minke whales, as well as humpbacks, which can be as long as 15m (50ft), and fin whales. Blue whales, orcas and sperm whales are sometimes seen, as are dolphins and porpoises.

road works in the street in 1992. The city has wisely protected it with a glass cover to make sure it doesn't suffer any further indignities.

Every weekend in the old customs building (Geirsgata, open all year Sat–Sun 11am–5pm; free) is the **Kolaportið Flea Market**. Alongside the usual array of bric-à-brac, second-hand books and clothes, there are stalls selling fish, both fresh and dried – unquestionable evidence that you are in Iceland. This is the place to try the traditional Icelandic snack of *hardfiskur*, literally hard fish. If you try to imagine Kettle Chips flavoured with cod then you'll have some idea what to expect.

Árnason's Sólfar suncraft

Sólfar Suncraft

Along the bay to the east of the harbour and well worth the walk is Jón Gunnar Árnason's 1986 stainless-steel sculpture *Sólfar suncraft*. It is very modern looking, but the shape of the Viking longboat on which it is based is easy to make out. It occupies an impressive spot looking out over the sea, although if you come from the city centre you may have to navigate your way across the busy Sæbraut coast road to get to it. A better way of approaching it is as part of a harbour walk from the quayside to the east. If the weather is clear there are great views across to Mt Esja on the other side of the bay.

WESTERN REYKJAVÍK

The western half of Reykjavík is a mainly residential area, but there are some important sights in this part of town nonetheless, and the reopening of the National Museum after years of closure is likely to put the west back on the tourist trail.

Starting from the City Hall and heading down the western side of Tjörnin, the first building of note is the government reception house **Ráðherrabústaðurinn** (closed to the public) at Tjarnargata 32. This fine old wooden building was originally constructed at Önundarfjördur in the West Fjords by a wealthy Norweigan businessman. He made a gift of it to

The National Museum

Iceland's first Home Rule government in 1904, and it is now used to put up visiting foreign dignitaries.

On Suðurgata is the oddly atmospheric Old Graveyard, inside which is a memorial to the independence leader, Jón Sigurðsson, as well as various Viking-style markers. Take a look at the headstones and you'll get an idea of how Icelandic names work and are recycled. There aren't that many variations and in the family plots you can see how a father's first name is passed on to his children as their surname *(see box page 13)*.

National Museum

At the far end of the cemetery, adjacent to a busy roundabout, is **Þjódminjasafn Íslands** (National Museum, Hringbraut, junction with Suðurgata; open all year Tues–Sun 10am–6pm, closes 5pm in winter; admission charge), which was shut for six years until it reopened in September 2004. The exhibition spaces cover 2,000 sq m (21,500 sq ft) and claims to be as up to date and well-equipped as any museum in the world. There is enough room for a substantial permanent collection to be displayed as well as two visiting exhibitions at any one time.

The museum is essentially dedicated to Icelandic history and culture from the first settlements to the present day. The results of the latest research, involving DNA from the bones of the earliest Icelanders, are used to help to trace where the population originated from. Graves from the early heathen period have been restored and put on display alongside archeological treasures that have been recovered from where they were buried by the eruption of the Hekla volcano in 1104. Religion and superstition play a big role in many of the oldest exhibits, which tell the story of witchcraft, the coming of Christianity and the conversion from paganism. The first Bible to be printed in Icelandic is on show as well as a complete medieval church.

The later history concentrates on the economic development of the country and its growing political emergence after centuries of foreign rule. Particularly interesting is the census of 1703, the first to record the entire population of Iceland, along with their livestock and details of their living conditions.

Nordic House

South, on the way to the domestic airport, is **Norræna Húsið** ◄ (Nordic House, Sturlugata 5; open daily noon–5pm, exhibitions closed Mon; admission charge for exhibitions only), a Scandinavian cultural centre with a well-stocked library

Inside Nordic House, a Scandinavian cultural centre

offering free internet access, exhibitions (including good photographic shows), concerts and a pleasant, relatively inexpensive cafe (open Mon–Fri 8am–5pm; Sat and Sun noon–5pm). Unless Nordic culture is your passion, you're likely to find the building itself more interesting than its contents. It was designed by the Finnish architect Alvar Aalto and is a fine example of early 1960s' modernism. Most of the events are conducted in one or other of the Nordic languages.

Öskjuhlíð and the Pearl

Also on the western edge of the city, although on the other side of the domestic airport, is a bizarre collection of buildings on a hill known as **Öskjuhlíð**. The hill – a British army base during World War II – has been reforested and is now a popular place for walking (there are tracks), cycling and, if the weather allows, sunbathing. Sitting on top of the hill, and providing a vantage point for many miles around, are six enormous tanks, the **Perlan** (Pearl), which are used to store the geothermally heated water that supplies the city. There's also a restaurant at the Perlan and a free viewing platform with splendid views across the city and the mountains beyond.

The high-tech Pearl

If you want to see what all those colourful characters in

the Saga stories were really like, then this is the place to come. Inside the building that also houses the Pearl's restaurant is the recently opened **Sögusafnið** (Saga Museum; open daily 10am–6pm; admission charge). This is history as pure theatre, with full-size models showing how the first Icelanders lived, the kind of boats they travelled in, and the gory ways in

Statues outside the Pearl

which many of them died. As soon as you step into the darkened gallery you are bombarded with the sights and sounds of battle. Nobody can be certain what the great figures of the Saga Era – Snorri, Erik the Red, Leifur Eiríksson et al – actually looked like, but the models here will give you a good idea.

The building also houses an impressive artificial geyser, just in case you don't have time to go out of the city to see a real one (*see page 62*). It shoots a jet of water up four floors and is much more regular than those powered by nature.

Nauthólsvík Geothermal Beach

At the southern edge of Öskjuhlíð is a geothermal beach, **Nauthólsvík** (free but charge for changing facilities), where the seawater is heated by the addition of hot water from the hill. The sea water reaches 20ºC (68ºF), and there's a hotpot that gets even hotter (up to 35ºC/95ºF.) If you like water sports, this is the place to come, as kayaks are available to hire, and it's the base of the Reykjavík Yacht Club. It's also a good spot for building sandcastles, using the wonderfully bright golden sand (a popular pastime with the local children). For refreshment, visit the pleasant cafe that looks out over the beach.

EASTERN REYKJAVÍK

On the eastern side of the city there's a stretch of museums and other sights between the centre and the large park, pool and zoo at Laugardalur.

Höfði

The first sight you come to in this part of town, located close to the sea and set alone on a grassy square, is **Höfði**, often known as the Reagan-Gorbachev House. The building is used as a venue for government receptions and other social functions and as a result is almost always closed to the public. It's an imposing-looking building, though, and when the two presidents came here in 1986 to discuss cutting nuclear weapons, it helped to put Iceland on the international map. This small corner of Reykjavík suddenly became the focus of attention for all the world's media, and the city had never seen anything like it. The summit broke down, with Mikhail Gorbachev blaming Ronald Reagan's insistence on keeping his Star Wars plans intact. The former US President's death in 2004 is likely to increase the popularity of this site, at least for American visitors.

Site of the 1986 summit: the Höfði

If international diplomacy isn't of interest to you, you

can always look through the windows and imagine the ghost of a young girl who supposedly haunts the house. She poisoned herself after being found guilty of incest and is said to spend her time switching on and off lights and knocking pictures off the walls. There is no record of the two presidents being troubled by her, but one British diplomat who stayed in the Höfði house was so unnerved that he demanded to be moved.

Natural History Museum

A couple of blocks southwest is **Náttúrufræðisafnið** (Museum of Natural History, Hverfisgata 116; open June–Aug Tues, Thur, Sat, Sun 1–5pm, Sept–May same days 1.30–4pm; admission charge). This scientific institution is staffed by a team of experts in every aspect of Icelandic flora and fauna. There are more than 9,000 books in the library, which is impressive for a country with no trees to speak of and very few indigenous species of animals. Many worthwhile conservation projects are run from here, including bird ringing and environmental protection projects.

The museum is quite academic and will probably only appeal to keen nature enthusiasts. Display cabinets show just about every fish, bird and bird's egg to be found in the region. Not all of them are conservation success stories, however. If you've ever wondered what the Great Auk looked like before it became extinct, you can see a stuffed one here *(see box)*. And the impressive giant leatherback turtle isn't native. It was washed up already dead in the West Fjords 40 years ago.

> **The Great Auk was hunted out of existence with the last two being killed on Eldey Island southwest of Reykjavík in 1844. Even stuffed examples of this unique flightless bird are rare. The one displayed in the Natural History Museum was bought in an auction at Sotheby's in London in 1971.**

Art showcased at the Kjarvalsstaðir

Kjarvalsstaðir

Further inland, set in a tree-lined park, is **Kjarvalsstaðir** (Municipal Gallery, Flóka-gata; open daily 10am–5pm, Wed 10am–7pm; admission charge except Mon). The building itself is something of an eyesore from the outside, but the exhibits inside are well worth the trek. Half the gallery is dedicated to the huge, colourful and often abstract landscapes by the Icelandic artist Jóhannes Kjarval (1885–1972); the other half houses visiting exhibitions of both paintings and photography. Outside, in the grounds, there's a little cafe.

Ásmundur Sveinsson Sculpture Museum

Keep going east to reach the **Ásmundursafn** (Asmundur Sveinsson Sculpture Museum, Sigtún; open daily May–Sept 10am–4pm, Oct–Apr 1–4pm; admission charge except Mon), which you can enter on the same ticket as Hafnar-húsið and Kjarvalsstaðir *(see pages 41 and above)*. This bright, airy gallery contains some examples of modern sculpture at its very best, with huge figures depicting the people of Iceland as well as mythical characters. Even if the museum is closed, the place is worth a visit, as some pieces are located in the wooded garden (free access).

Sigurjón Ólafsson Museum

There is more sculpture and some notable 20th-century por-traits in the **Safn Sigurjóns Ólafssonar** (Sigurjón Ólafsson

Museum, Laugarnestangi 70; open Jun–Aug Tues–Sun 2–5pm; Sept–May Sat–Sun 2–5pm; admission charge). From June to August on Tuesday evenings at 8.30pm there are concerts here (most are classical with some jazz and other genres).

Laugardalur

A short distance to the east, across a busy dual carriageway, is **Laugardalur**, a huge free park that houses a large sports stadium, swimming pool, botanical garden and zoo. The 50-m (165-ft) thermal pool is the largest in the city, and there are hot pots, a sauna and a steam room, too, providing an ideal way in which to relax. Alongside the pool complex are acres of well-kept parkland, and in the gardens at the eastern edge you can see most of the range of Icelandic plants as well as a large number of imported varieties. Other attractions in the park include a Viking-themed children's playground and a go-cart track.

The swimming pool at Laugardalur

The Zoo

The spacious and well-run **Húsdýragarðurinn** (Reykjavík Family Park and Zoo; open May–Sept daily 10am–6pm; admission charge) showcases animal species found in Iceland itself, such as arctic fox, minx, seals and reindeer, plus farmyard and domestic animals including Icelandic horses, cattle, sheep, pigs, goats, hens, dogs and cats. There are about 150 animals in all, from almost 20 species, and care is taken to include variations of colour, age and gender. Feeding times for the various animals are posted up at the entrance.

Árbær Open-Air Museum

A short bus or taxi journey further east takes you to the **Árbæjarsafn** (Árbær Open-Air Museum; open June–Aug Mon 11am–4pm, Tues–Fri 9am–5pm, Sat, Sun 10am–6pm; admission charge). The original farm was mentioned in the Sagas

Watching the penguins at the zoo

and is now a showcase for how Icelanders used to live. Here, there are old homesteads with turf roofs from all around the country and a church that dates from 1842. Most of the houses are from Reykjavík, however, and the oldest house was built in 1820. The museum shows how Reykjavík has grown

> **Iceland isn't quite as cold as it sounds. The Gulf Stream keeps temperatures moderate all year round. Even in winter it doesn't snow much in Reykjavík. Average January temperatures are around zero, higher than those in New York.**

from little more than a hamlet to the city it is today. The buildings are added to on a regular basis, as the collection expands. There are also exhibitions of toys and other family items and on the development of public transport and other services in the capital. The helpful staff, most of them dressed in period clothes, will help to guide you round the exhibition.

HAFNARFJÖRÐUR

Although technically a town in its own right, Hafnarfjörður is really a suburb of the capital, albeit one that has developed a separate tourist industry. The bus from the international airport at Keflavík stops here in both directions and there's more than enough to do to justify breaking your journey for half a day. The location is attractive, with big open parks up on the cliff tops, and you get a greater sense of being out in the North Atlantic than you do in Reykjavík itself. On a clear day there are great views of the city centre from the higher parts of the town.

Viking Village

The main tourist spot in Hafnarfjörður is at **Fjörukráin** (Viking Village, Strandgata 50a; open all year noon–10pm, free). You can't miss it due to the carved dragon-like creatures on the roof and the tall wooden sculpture outside.

The village is mainly a place to eat, drink and, possibly, spend the night – there's a guesthouse and two dining areas (one a banqueting hall and the other an outdoor tented camp, where the waiters are dressed as Vikings). If you fancy splashing out, you can enjoy a full banquet of traditional Icelandic fare, in quantities sufficient to set you up for any amount of marauding and pillage.

Museums and Galleries

Just north of the harbour, the **Hafnarfjörður Museum** (Pakkhusið, Vesturgata 8; open daily, June–Aug 1–5pm, Sept–May Sat, Sun only 1–5pm; admission charge) contains a potted history of the town with emphasis on its seafaring traditions while next door at No. 6, **Sívertsens-Húsið** (same times as above; admission charge) is a fine example of an old merchant's house, dating from 1803 and the oldest building in Hafnarfjörður. South of the harbour is the **Menningor og Listastofnun Hafnarfjarðar** (Hafnarborg Institute of Culture and Fine Art, Strandgata 34; open Wed–Mon noon–6pm; admission charge), with a permanent collection and changing exhibitions by Icelandic and international artists. Occasional music recitals and other events are

Hafnarfjörður's oldest house

also held here. There is a fine church and sculpture garden at Viðistaðir on the northern outskirts of the town.

Outdoor Attractions

One of the best ways to get a feel for Hafnarfjörður is to do one of the **Sculpture and Shore Walks** or perhaps the **Elf Walk**. Start at the tourist office on Vesturgata, where you can get details of routes. There's no guarantee that you'll spot any elves, or even the ancient hermit who supposedly lives here, but you can be more certain of great views and plenty of bird life.

Hellisgerdi Park (Nönnustígur; open all year; free) is where the elves and the hermit apparently hang out, and there's also a bonsai garden here, which may be where the little 'hidden people' hide from the tourists.

South of Hafnarfjörður is **Ástjörn Nature Reserve**. Attractively located on the side of a lake, it features what is claimed to be Iceland's smallest mountain and abundant bird life.

Chess

Reykjavík played host to what has been called 'the most extraordinary chess match of all time' in 1972. The American Bobby Fischer played the reigning world champion, Boris Spassky, from the former USSR. It was a Cold War battle over the chess board. Fischer was accused of being so desperate to win that he used psychological intimidation to destroy Spassky's morale. It was so intense that the Icelandic authorities and the World Chess Federation were at a loss as to what to do about it. Fischer won but the suspicion lasted that his tantrums and ultimatums amounted to cheating. One American player said of Fischer that 'if he wasn't a chess player he might have been a dangerous psychopath'. He went on to become an increasingly erratic recluse. The affection of the people of Reykjavík for chess survived, however, and it remains a very popular game in Iceland.

Icelandic horses – a familiar sight in the fields around Reykjavík

EXCURSIONS

Even if you plan to spend most of your visit to Iceland in Reykjavík, you should try to make time for one of the day trips to the extraordinary sights just outside the capital – to the so-called Golden Circle *(see page 59)* or to the Blue Lagoon *(see page 65)*, as no visit to Reykjavík is really complete without seeing a geyser spurting boiling water into the air or luxuriating in the world-famous health spa. Whale-watching trips and bird-spotting tours to islands including Viðey are also widely advertised from the capital.

If you have a little more time, you could try heading further afield, whether along the south coast to Vík or west to the Snæfellnes Peninsula. Thanks to the relatively cheap and extremely efficient domestic air services, a short flight either north to Akureyri *(see page 79)* or south to the Westman Islands *(see page 68)* can make for a fascinating day trip. All the places listed in this section feature as one-day excursions run by the major tour companies *(see Tours, page 128)* and can also be organised independently.

For a full picture of suitable destinations for longer trips away from the capital see the *Berlitz Guide Iceland*.

The Golden Circle

This 200-km (125-mile) round trip from Reykjavík takes in some of the key historical and geological sites in Iceland including the original geyser that gave its name to gushing blowholes worldwide, the site of Iceland's first parliament, and one of the country's most dramatic waterfalls. You can cover the full route on any one of a number of day tours from Reykjavík. These tours take approximately seven hours, but they do include stops at gift shops and eating places along the way. Most hotels offer a variety of different excursions talking in all or just some of the sights. The trip can just about be done by public transport (in season, ie June–August only, *see Tours, page 128*) or you could hire a car. The route is well signposted, and parking is good.

Þingvellir

The nearest of the Golden Circle sites to the capital is the place where Iceland's original Alþingi (parliament) was established in 930. It is situated in **Þingvellir** (Assembly Plains; admission free), a large national park that has enormous political and geographical significance and was declared a UNESCO World Heritage site in 2004. Unfortunately, there are only a few actual monuments and buildings to be

> The park is situated on top of the line where the two continental plates of North America and Europe meet. In fact they are slowly moving apart, widening Iceland by 1.5cm (⅝in) a year.

seen, so you have to use your imagination a little to picture the events of the past. However, there is a helpful information and education centre with videos and maps explaining the historical significance of the site. Fishing and camping permits can also be obtained here.

Outside the building are several maps and billboards explaining the best routes to explore the area. It's worth familiarising yourself with the layout of the area before you set off to explore, as the park itself is not that well signposted. From this viewing point, you have good views of the rift valley, where the two continental plates of North America and Europe meet *(see box, page 59)*, as you look towards the lake.

The most obvious landmark at Þingvellir is the red-roofed church, which dates from 1859 and stands on the site of a much bigger church that held sway over all the local inhabitants in the 18th century. The first church was built here by

Views over Þingvellir, on a fine day

the King of Norway, Ólafur Haraldsson, in the early years of the settlement c.1018, and there's evidence that the site was in use even earlier. At the back of the current church is a site reserved for the burial of notable Icelanders, although

Alþingi's last meeting was held on this site in 1798; in 1800 its authority was abolished. A national court and parliament was founded in Reykjavík, which then had a population of 300.

only two tombs have been allowed so far – both for patriotic poets. The buildings alongside the church house a school and the home of the church warden.

It may not be immediately obvious, but below you is the Alþingi site itself. You can walk down into it and get your bearings from a flagpole that marks the approximate spot from which the leader of the parliament, the law speaker, made his proclamations. From here the rift wall, called Almannagjá, rises up in front of you. To the right of the flagpole, as you face the rift wall, is a plaque and part of the walls from an 18th-century meeting house, or *buð* (literally 'booth'), used by participants at the assembly.

If you have time, the surrounding park is well worth a stroll. Just to the east of the Alþingi the Öxará River flows over the rift wall and into a lake, Þingvallavatn. The waterfall here is the 20-m (66-ft) Öxaráfoss. Nearby you can clearly see the layers of ash left by successive eruptions over the centuries. It's thought that the river was diverted to its present course when the Alþingi was first established in order to provide water for the participants. For a while pools along the river were used for executing alleged witches. On the opposite side of the river from the church there are more *buð* sites along the bank, and a deep pool created by seismic activity is now a wishing well full of coins from all over the world.

Skálholt

Next stop on the Golden Circle is the church at **Skálholt**, about 45km (28 miles) to the east of Þingvellir, a seat of ecclesiastical, rather than political, power. Skálholt was the site of a bishopric from 1056 until a massive earthquake destroyed its cathedral in the late 18th century. The bishop picked up his cassock and headed for the relative safety of Reykjavík, and it wasn't until 1963 that the present church was finally restored and reconsecrated. It's hard to imagine when you see the church that it was once at the centre of the biggest settlement in Iceland and site of the country's first school. Inside you can see the coffin of one of the early bishops, uncovered during the reconstruction work, and a fine modern mosaic above the altar. Alongside the church there is a conference and cultural centre, where concerts and art exhibitions are staged in summer

► *Geysir*

Another 20km (12½ miles) to the northeast you can see evidence of the one power that both church and state have to respect: nature. There are bigger geysers (*geysir* in Icelandic) in the world, and more impressive ones too, but this is the site of the original – *geysir* is the one Icelandic word to have made it into the lexicon of world language. Sadly, the gusher that used to shoot 70m (230ft) into the air now does nothing more than gurgle. It first spurted during the 14th century, but has

Blesi, one of the numerous boiling pools at Geysir

been mostly inactive since the 1960s. For years Icelanders poured masses of soap powder into the orifice, a sort of Viagra for geysers, to make it perform, but in the end they gave up, apart from on very special occasions, such as Independence Day. (The English poet W.H. Auden noted in the 1930s that Icelanders were already using imported liquid Sunlight soap – the thinner local type did not work – to encourage Geysir to explode.) Even then, there are no guarantees that the great geyser will perform. If it does, the spume can hit 60m (200ft).

Watching Strokkur spurt into the air at Geysir

In the light of this, many people were stunned when Geysir suddenly erupted in June 2001, seemingly quite out of the blue. Water spouted up to 40m (130ft) into the air, and the activity continued periodically over several weeks. However, this extraordinary occurrence had a perfectly rational explanation: earthquakes in Southern Iceland caused subterranean pressure that gave the great Geysir renewed vitality.

Fortunately, right beside Geysir there is the smaller, but considerably more reliable, **Strokkur** (literally 'the churn'), which spurts to a most impressive height of around 20m (66ft) every few minutes, without any artificial encouragement. Never stand too close to Strokkur, however, as the water is exceedingly hot – an average of seven tourists are scalded every week during the summer months, mostly as a result of putting their hands in the water pools that surround this geyser to test the temperature.

The whole Geysir area is geothermically active and smells strongly of sulphur (similar to the smell of a rotten egg). You should stick to the walking trails that are marked out among the steaming vents and glistening, multicoloured mud formations.

Gullfoss

An example of nature at its most forceful is to be found another 6km (3¾ miles) along the road to the north. **Gullfoss** (Golden Falls) is, in fact, two separate waterfalls a short distance apart. Their combined drop is 32m (105ft), and the canyon below is some 2km (1¼ miles) long, with basalt

Gullfoss is one of Iceland's most impressive waterfalls

columns that look like the pipes of an organ rising up from the bottom. Trails climb past the waterfall's northern face, allowing you to get within an arm's length of the awesome flow. Wear a raincoat, or be prepared for the clouds of spray that create photogenic rainbows on sunny days to douse you from head to foot. (The effect is less spectacular on cold, grey days, when you are likely to feel somewhat battered by the elements.)

The falls were nearly destroyed by a hydroelectric dam project in the 1920s, but on that occasion the protests of ordinary Icelanders suceeded and now the area is protected. A stone plaque near the parking area remembers Sigríður Tómasdóttir, a farmer's daughter who lived on the nearby farm Brattholt. Private plans had been drawn up to dam the Hvítá river at Gullfoss for a hydroelectric project, but Sigríður walked to Reykjavík to protest to the government and even announced that she would fling herself into the waterfalls if construction went ahead. The government instead bought the falls and made them a national monument.

Another path leaving from the parking area climbs to the top of the surrounding cliffs for a panoramic view of the falls. From Gullfoss, the road stretches ahead into the uninhabited deserts of central Iceland, and on a clear day you can see the icecap Langjökull ('long glacier').

The Blue Lagoon

One trip out of Reykjavík that really should not be missed is to the world's greatest outdoor bath, **Bláa Lonið** (Blue Lagoon, Grindavík, tel: 420 8800; <www.bluelagoon.com>; open daily mid-May–Aug 9am–9pm, Sept–mid-May 10am–7.30pm; admission charge). Most hotels will have details of tours, but it is cheaper to make your own way there and it is easily done by public transport. There are several buses a day out here from the main bus station in Reykjavík. It's not far from the international airport at Keflavík, so it can also be a stopping-off point on the way home.

The lagoon itself is a pool of seawater naturally heated by the geothermal activity below the surface. It sits in the middle of a lava field, and the water rises up through holes in the muddy bottom, so you can lounge around here with warm mud oozing between your toes in water temperatures of 36–39°C (97–102°F) all year round. The lagoon filled up next to the adjacent Svartsengi power station after the construction of the latter in the 1970s. People started to bathe here, and patients with skin complaints reported significant improvements in their condition, so official public bathing facilities were opened in 1987. An outpatients' clinic for psoriasis patients was later added. The water contains a mixture of salts, silica and blue-green algae, which is said to cleanse and soften the skin and relax the body.

The facilities here have been greatly improved in recent years, with a new visitors reception and restaurant and a modern shower block added. You are now barely aware of the adjacent power station. Two saunas have been built alongside the lagoon, and for an extra fee you can have a massage and be rubbed with some of the many Blue Lagoon products – said to enhance your energy flow and do wonders for body and soul – on sale in the gift shop.

The Blue Lagoon is officially recognised as a psoriasis clinic by the Icelandic Ministry of Health, and patients come to soak up its benefits from all over the world. Sufferers can receive a unique natural treatment based on bathing in the lagoon's geothermal seawater, while its unique active ingredients – mineral salts, silica and algae – exert their positive effects on the skin.

Whether you believe the hype or not, wallowing

Bathing in the famously therapeutic waters of the Blue Lagoon

about in the hot water for an hour or so should leave you feeling fantastic – and you can spread as much mud over your body as you like for free. Watch out for hot spots in the water, which can be too close to boiling point for comfort – you should, however, come upon them gradually and then be able to move away. Take care going down the steps into the lagoon, as they can be slippery and you could have a hard landing on the rocks lurking in the mud under the water. If you are in the lagoon at the end of the day you can watch the sun set while you soak away life's strains. Bathing suits, towels and bath robes can be hired at the reception.

Viðey

Just 1km (⅔ mile) out to sea due north of Reykjavík is the island of **Viðey**, a small but historically significant place, known mostly nowadays for its bird life. Sea birds, ducks and waders are all frequently seen here. Just up from the jetty is the oldest building in Iceland, Viðeyjarstofa, built in 1755 and now a classy restaurant. The island is small enough to cover easily on foot in an hour or two, and there are some impressive basalt columns on the isthmus at its centre. Ferries depart from Sundahöfn harbour in Reykjavík between June and September (for times, tel: 581 1010); the trip takes less than 10 minutes.

Akurey

One of the best places to see puffins close to the capital is on the tiny island of **Akurey**. You can't go ashore, but ferries depart from Reykjavík harbour between late May and August for an hour-long round-the-island trip. Tickets are available from the Reykjavík tourist office at Aðalstræti 2.

The Westman Islands

The **Westman Islands** – or Vestmannaeyjar to give them their Icelandic name – are in fact a long strip of 15 islands and numerous rocks lying approximately 10km (6 miles) off the south coast of Iceland. There are daily flights there and back from Reykjavík's domestic airport, and ferries leave from Þorlákshöfn south of the capital.

> **Get a weather forecast before setting off for the Westman Islands – it is not uncommon for the clouds and rain to descend by the middle of the afternoon, closing off the airport. The islands' hotels make good money out of people who find themselves stranded there.**

Carbon dating has suggested that the Westman Islands may have been the first part of Iceland to be inhabited. They were created by underwater eruptions, and the process is still going on: the newest island, Surtsey, emerged from the sea as recently as the mid-1960s. This little island has been studied with fascination by

The Westman Islands, possibly the first inhabited part of Iceland

scientists, not only because of its dramatic appearance from under the waves, but also for the flora and fauna that are taking root and making it their home.

The tourist authorities describe the Westman Islands as the 'Capri of the North', although even they wouldn't claim this had anything to do with the weather. The coves and inlets may be reminiscent of the chic Italian island, but the rain and wind that batter them for much of the year certainly are not.

Heimaey

The only inhabited Westman island is Heimaey, also home to the airport. Heimaey has a pretty little town of the same name, but most visitors come for the surrounding country-side and bird cliffs. Hundreds of thousands of puffins, as well as guillemots, fulmars and 30 other types of seabird come here every year to nest and breed on the precipitous cliffs. You can reach them on foot or take a boat out and get a better view from the sea. You might also see whales and seals in the waters around the islands. (Keikó, the killer whale that starred in the Hollywood film *Free Willy* lived in the harbour here for a few years after a public campaign in the US to have him returned to the wild. He was later moved on to Norway where he eventually died.)

The other big draw of Heimaey is the landscape. Two dramatic cones rise up just outside the town: the volcano, Helgafell, and a much newer mountain, Eldfell, which was created as a result of a massive eruption in 1973 that almost buried the town.

In the early hours of 23 January 1973 a fissure nearly 2-km (1¼-mile) long opened up on the eastern side of Helgafell. Red hot lava started to spurt into the sky heralding an eruption that was to last for the next six months. The threat to the town was immediate, and the entire 5,000-strong population was taken off to the mainland. Flying bombs of molten lava crashed through windows or melted through roofs, and a colossal river of lava made its way towards the town. Many houses collapsed under the weight of falling ash

Puffins

The puffin is a national symbol in Iceland as well as a national dish. It is a member of the auk family and has a multicoloured beak and bright orange legs and feet. Puffins are highly sociable, often standing about in groups and nesting in large colonies. They fish together, too, forming wide rafts out to sea. They can dive to 60m (200ft) in search of fish, but also eat plankton in winter. They rarely travel far from their colony while raising their young. Both parents incubate a single egg. The males and females look very similar, but neither grow much more than 30cm (12in) in height. They produce a dark meat, like tastes like duck but is less fatty, and is often served with a fruity sauce.

The puffin is the national symbol of Iceland

and by the time the flow had stopped a quarter of Heimaey had been destroyed.

The harbour was saved at the last minute, and to this day nobody is sure whether this was just luck or whether the millions of tons of seawater that the emergency services poured onto the advancing river of rock did the trick. Either way the harbour had a new wall and much better protection from the elements.

When it was all over, the island was 2.2 sq km (½ sq mile) larger, and the new mountain of Eldfell had been created. Every day in summer, a film, the *Volcano Show*, which including some dramatic footage of the eruption, is aired in the town centre.

Around the island there are numerous walks to be enjoyed, the most impressive of which is off to the west coast and the valley of Herjólfsdalur. Venture a little further and you will reach some of Heimaey's best bird cliffs, where you can get remarkably close to the puffins.

The South Coast

Þórsmörk and Skógar

A recent addition to day tours from Reykjavík is a trip to **Þórsmörk** (Thor's Wood), where you'll get a real sense of the majesty of the Icelandic terrain. It is set in a beautiful valley with outstanding views, and city dwellers from Reykjavík flock here at weekends to enjoy the wooded walks, flora and fauna and lovely views. To get to Þórsmörk you have to skirt Mt Hekla, the second most active volcano in the country, and you will soon find yourself surrounded by glaciers and little more than wilderness.

Traditional homestead in Skógar

You are now entering Saga country and, in particular, the setting for the most bloody of the sagas – that which tells the story of the wise and decent Njál and the gruesome end met by most of his friends and family. Much of the action took place at the Alþingi at Þingvellir *(see page 59)*, but there was more than a little blood-letting near the village of **Hvolsvöllur** where there is now an Icelandic Saga Centre with background information on the various tales. Here, there is a turning northeast that will take you up to Þórsmörk itself.

East of Þórsmörk is **Skógar**, home to a meticulously

managed folk museum (open daily; June–Aug 9am–7pm, May and Sept 10am–5pm; admission charge), the most visited of its kind in Iceland. In addition to a fine 6,000-piece collection, the museum showcases different Icelandic housing through the ages.

> **For those with sufficient time to explore the island, there are two main routes that go right across the interior – the Kjölur and the Sprengisandur. Coaches run from Reykjavík.**

There is a summer Edda Hotel at Skógar, as well as the splendid waterfall, **Skógafoss**, the sheer drop of which offers one of south Iceland's best photo opportunities. The trek from here to Þórsmörk, passing between the ice-caps of Eyjafjallajökull and Mýrdalsjökull over the Fimmvörðuháls pass, is popular with the hardy between June and September, so much so that it becomes quite crowded, particularly in July. There are two huts between the ice-caps: one is an emergency shelter; the other is pre-bookable.

North of Þórsmörk is **Landmannalaugar**, part of the Fjallabak Nature Reserve and a good base for the many walks in the area (there are camping and hut facilities here). Landmannalaugar's spectacular rhyolitic hills are bright yellow, green and red, dotted with deep blue lakes, creamy brown plains and snow patches on grey mosses. There are hot springs here, and steam rises from patches of ground across the valley.

Vík

Back on the ring road and heading east you will reach the coastal town of Vík or, to give it its full name, **Vík í Mýrdal** (Bay of the Marshy Valley). It's a pretty little town, with a symbol of a smiling yellow face that greets you everywhere – possibly to try to counter its reputation as the rainiest place in Iceland. Most people come here for the black volcanic sand, cliffs and bird life. Three steeples of stone, known as

Vík's 'Troll Rocks'

➤ **Reynisdrangar** (Troll Rocks), rise out of the sea. Legend has it they are the figures of trolls that turned to stone when they failed to get under cover before the sun hit them. Whatever their origin, in summer they teem with bird life, including kitti-wakes, Arctic tern, puffins, gannets and guillemots.

The West Coast

The drive immediately north of Reykjavík is, on the whole, less rewarding than heading south and east, at least to start with. However, there are some very significant historical and cultural sights to be seen a little further out, and if you have time to go as far as the **Snæfellsnes Peninsula** you will be able to experience the scenery in one of the most dramatic parts of the country. Two things in particular bring visitors to the peninsula: the extinct volcano, **Snæfellsjökull**, and whale-watching tours from **Ólafsvík**. On the way, there there are a few attractions to help to break up the journey, too.

Akranes

Located just north of Reykjavík, **Akranes** is dominated by fish-processing, trawler production and cement making. Fortunately, it is also home to the excellent **Safnasvæðið á Akranesi** (Akranes Folk Museum; open May–Aug daily 10.30am–noon and 1.30–4.30pm, Sept–Apr Mon–Fri 1.30–4.30pm; admission charge), on the eastern side of town. There are exhibits from both the land and sea, including trawler-wire cutters from the Cod Wars with Britain in the 1970s and a well-preserved ketch, one of the first decked fishing boats in Iceland. There are also displays marking Iceland's sporting achievements and the country's largest collection of rocks, minerals and fossils.

The town also has a great **swimming pool complex** (Garðabraut, open all year Mon–Fri 6.45am–9pm; Sat and Sun 9am–6pm; admission charge), with a steam room and four hotpots. Behind the pool buildings there is also a long sandy beach called Langisandur, which faces south and enjoys plenty of sun when the clouds make way for it. If you want to swim, however, you would be well advised to stick to the pool, as the sea temperature rarely gets above 5°C (41°F).

Borgarnes

The attractions in the town of **Borgarnes** won't delay you for long. Of greatest interest is its setting, with views over two impressive glaciers in one direction and a fjord in the other. Borgarnes can just about claim to be a Saga site. Egill Skallagrímsson gave his name to *Egill's Saga,* and his talents ran to piracy, general unpleasantness and, surprisingly, poetry. In the town, there's a statue, not of Egill himself but of his father and Egill's drowned son; their burial mound can be seen nearby. Other attractions include a museum, **Safnahús Borgarfjardar** (Borgarfjordur Cultural Centre, Borgarbraut; open June–Aug daily 1–6pm; admission charge), and a good open-air pool.

Beacon on the cliffs

Reykholt

Reykholt is without doubt the highlight of this stretch of the coast north of Reykjavík. It's a little way inland from the coast road but well worth the detour. Snorri Sturluson lived here for rather longer than he did at Borg, and the musem is a very accessible summary both of his work and the other Sagas. It stands alongside a very attractive church, and the priest is a genuine expert on Iceland's cultural history. Down beside the museum (Heimskringla; open daily June–Aug; 10am–6pm; admission charge) is the pool where Snorri bathed, Snorralaug. You can see the remains of the tunnel that led to his farmhouse and the place where he was assassinated in 1241 after getting mixed up in Norweigan royal rivalries.

Deildartunguhver

Between Reykholt and the coast is the largest hot spring in Europe. Over 180 litres of almost boiling water gurgle to the surface every second, sending clouds of steam up into the air. The towns of Akranes and Borgarnes are both heated from this hot water supply. There's a fence to keep you from getting too close to the water, but be warned that people are scalded occasionally when a particularly strong gush of water splashes across the pathway.

The Snæfellsnes Peninsula

After the well-maintained roads of Reykjavík and the ring-road north, branching out onto the Snæfellsnes Peninsula is quite an experience. You quickly get the sense of being off the beaten track, and the roads here can be very windy and bumpy. However, the views are exceptional, so don't be deterred. You can do a circuit of the peninsula in a day or choose between visiting the glacier in the west or the attractive fishing town of Stykkishólmur to the north.

The glacier at **Snæfellsjökull** covers an extinct volcano and at 1,445m (4,740ft) high it is permanently snow-capped. The place was made famous by Jules Verne as the entry point for his novel *Journey to the Centre of the Earth*. It also plays a role in *Under the Glacier* by Nobel Prize-winning Icelandic novelist Halldór Laxness *(see box, page 78)*. The main peak itself is a less daunting climb than it looks, but only experienced climbers should attempt it, as the weather is always a danger here. The glacier is popular for snow-mobile tours.

Further round the peninsula is **Ólafsvík**, where whale-watching tours (daily June–Aug; book with Eyja-ferdir, tel: 438 1450, or the tourist office, tel: 436 1543) leave by catamaran. This is the best place to spot killer whales, humpbacks and, if you're lucky, the massive blue whale. Ólafsvík itself is a peaceful but highly productive little fishing town, with attractions including a church, Kirkjutún, with a

Hardy Icelandic sheep

strange three-legged tower off to the side, and the town's small folk museum (open daily late May–Aug; 9am–7pm; admission charge). Ólafsvík is also notable as the birthplace of one of Iceland's most prominent creatives, the pop artist Erró (born in 1932 as Gundmundur Ferró).

Stykkishólmur can be reached by carrying on along the coast road. If you decide to skip the glacier, you can get here via a shorter route directly north across the peninsula. It is an attractive town with brightly painted wooden houses down by the harbour. It's famous for its scallops and halibut, and at the quayside it's possible to take a two-hour bird-watching and scallop-tasting tour. There is an unusual modern church overlooking the town with a roof brightly illuminated with thousands of tiny bulbs. Classical music concerts take place here on Sundays in summer (admission charge).

Halldór Laxness

The most important modern literary figure in Iceland is Halldór Kiljan Laxness (1902–98), winner of the 1955 Nobel Prize for Literature. Laxness broke away from the idealisation of peasant life prevalent in Icelandic writing, portraying the dark underside of rural life, which caused resentment amongst those who felt he was presenting Iceland in a bad light. But, in his own way, Laxness was as fervent a patriot as any. His novel *Bell of Iceland*, set in the 18th century, contains references to the contemporary independence struggle. The postwar *Atom Station*, from the time of the NATO airbase controversy, contains pointed criticism of the politicians who were ready to sign away their country's independence out of greed. His best-known creation is Bjartur of Summerhouses, the peasant crofter hero of *Independent People*. Stubborn, infuriating but 'the most independent man in the country', Bjartur has come to represent the archetypal Icelander. Laxness's best work, *World Light*, is a trilogy dealing with the poet's role in society.

Houses in Stykkishólmur

South of the town, Helgafell ('holy mountain') – much talked about in Icelandic folklore – is little more than a hillock. However, it is said that you can have three wishes granted if you climb it from the west in silence and then descend to the east without looking back.

Akureyri, Capital of the North

Many visitors to Reykjavík try to make at least one trip away from the capital and the immediate area surrounding it. One option is to take a flight to Iceland's second city, **Akureyri**, on the north coast. There are regular flights from the domestic airport in Reykjavík, and the fares are far from prohibitive. If you are in Reykjavík on a cruise, there's a good chance that you will also be taken up to Akureyri as part of the package.

Akureyri is generally considered to be the capital of the north, and prides itself on having many of the attractions of a much bigger city in a uniquely attractive setting. The coastline is dramatic, and there are some huge fjords nearby – a feature that is almost completely lacking in the south. Akureyri is surrounded by high mountains, which are up to 1,500m (4,920ft) tall and snowcapped for much of the year. Thanks to its agreeable climate, it is green and lush compared with Reykjavík.

The main shopping street is the pedestrianised **Hafnarstræti**, which runs from close to the huge main church (*see below*) towards the rather nondescript town square, Ráðhústorg. Running east from the square is Strandgata, which has become the trendy corner of town; this leads down to the port, where cruise liners dock in summer.

The church steeples of the **Akureyrarkirkja** (open all year; daily 10am–noon and 2–4pm; free) tower over the city and are most dramatic at night when spotlit against the dark sky. Inside is a fine stained-glass window from the original cathedral at Coventry in the English Midlands. The window was removed at the start of World War II before the cathedral was destroyed by bombs; it was rescued from a London antiques shop and now forms the centrepiece of an impressive display that also features scenes from Iceland's own history.

The town's other main attractions include the **Lystigarðurinn** (Botanical Gardens; Eyrarlandsvegur; open June–Oct Mon–Fri 8am–10pm, Sat and Sun 9am–10pm; free). It's a tribute to the milder weather in this part of Iceland that so many species from all around the world are able to survive in the open air. There are plants in these gardens from southern Europe, Africa, South America and Aus-

Despite being closer to the Arctic Circle than Reykjavík, Akureyri has considerably better weather. Temperatures in the town can reach a balmy 20°C (68°F) or more in summer.

tralasia, as well as examples of just about every variety that grows in Iceland.

Be sure not to miss the excellent **Ainjasafnið a Akureyri** (Akureyri Municipal Museum, Aðalstræti 58; open daily June–mid-Sept 11am– 5pm, mid-Sept–May 2–4pm; admission charge), which is especially notable for its collection of everyday items dating to the 9th-century settlement. Among the collection is a beautifully painted pulpit.

Listasafn Akureyrar (Akureyri Art Museum, Kaupvangsstræti 24; open all year Tues–Sun 2–6pm, Fri, Sat until 10pm; free) showcases the talents of a wide range of local painters as well as hosting international exhibitions in the summer.

The town's **swimming pool** (Þingvallastræti 2; open daily 1–9pm; admission charge) is one of the best in the country, with facilities including a waterslide, sauna, steam room and hot tubs. Attached is a family park with mini-golf, electric cars and other attractions.

The Akureyrarkirkja by night

Akureyri was the childhood home of the Jesuit priest and author of the Nonni children's books, Jón Sveinsson. At Aðalstræti 54 you can visit the pretty wooden house he once lived in, **Nonnahús** (open June– Aug daily 10am–5pm; admission charge). His books have been translated into around 40 languages.

WHAT TO DO

That a country with a population of less than 300,000 (half of whom live in Reykjavík itself) has an internationally famed nightlife scene, three professional theatre companies, a thriving film industry, a national ballet, opera and symphony orchestra and hosts an international arts festival every other year is itself remarkable. Add to this the two dozen or so museums and galleries in Reykjavík, a jazz band that has made it into the UK charts and a world-class female pop star – can anywhere else match Iceland and its capital for variety and intensity of cultural activity in such a small community?

For those with time to venture outside Reykjavík, there can be few better places in the world for exploring the great outdoors, with many activities easily accessible from the capital. Hiking, skiing, snowmobiling and four-wheel-drive expeditions are all popular. Horseriding, birdwatching, whale-watching and white-water rafting also bring many visitors to Iceland.

NIGHTLIFE

In the 1990s Reykjavík developed an almost legendary reputation for its fashionable bars and clubs, though the nightlife scene was always somewhat overhyped due to the lack of knowledge about Iceland beyond the country's borders and the Icelanders' own formidable talent for self-publicism. While it is most definitely possible to have an extremely good night out

Beer was illegal throughout Iceland until 1989. On 1 March every year Reykjavík now celebrates 'Beer Day', when bars and clubs across the city arrange special events to mark the end of prohibition, which lasted some 75 years.

DJ Jo Lively

on the town, it's worth remembering that the city can be rather provincial and nightlife somewhat limited in scope when compared with other larger capital cities.

Bars and Cafes

There are, however, dozens of very welcoming bars and cafes for a drink or light meal during the evening, but the serious clubbing doesn't start until well after midnight. Reykjavíkers tend to dress up to go out, and there can be long queues outside the most fashionable places on Friday and Saturday. There is usually an admission charge of at least 1,000 Ikr, and drinks inside don't come cheap.

Brennivín: Icelandic fire water

As with most cities, clubs and pubs open and close in Reykjavík all the time, so it's worth asking around to find out where the newest and most fashionable places are. Publications such as *Netið Info Information for Tourists* and *What's On in Reykjavík* are good starting points. Some of the best clubs and bars that have been around for quite a while include **Nasa** (Austurvöllur), **Hverfisbarinn** (Hverfisgata 20), **Gaukur** á Stöng (Tryggvagata 22), **Café Victor** (Hafnarstræti 1–3), **Kaffi Reykjavík** (Vesturgata 2) and **Kaffibarin** (Bergstadastraeti 1), which is part owned by Blur's Damon Albarn.

Music, Theatre, Ballet

For more cultural nights out, Reykjavík has its own ballet, opera, symphony orchestra and several theatre and dance groups. *What's On in Reykjavík* and local papers list the latest shows. All the productions at the main professional theatres are in Icelandic, but often they are stagings of famous works with which tourists may be familiar.

Reykjavík has many stylish bars

Opera and dance, of course, transcend the language barrier. The Icelandic Opera is a world-class professional company, featuring top performers. The Icelandic Dance Company has in the past few years focused exclusively on modern dance. It is made up of both Icelandic and international dancers and has toured extensively abroad.

Jazz venues include Kaffileikhúsið (Café Theatre, Vesturgata 3) and the restaurant Jazz at Jómfrúin (Lækjargata 4), which has jazz recitals in summer (Sat 4–6pm).

Film

Although Reykjavík has a thriving film-making industry, eight out of ten films shown in the capital are American, screened with the original soundtrack and subtitles in Icelandic. On average, however, Icelanders go to the cinema 5.4 times a year, which is more often than any other nation in the world.

There are seven cinemas in the capital, plus a large film festival held in Reykjavík every two years, as well as the occasional smaller festival of alternative or artistic films. Check *Around Reykjavík* or *What's On* for details.

SHOPPING

Fashions, Laugavegur

Reykjavík isn't a shoppers' paradise, although it does have some interesting local outlets, and a tax-free shopping scheme helps to mitigate the otherwise high prices *(see opposite)*. The city does, however, have a good selection of trendy fashion shops for both sexes that are worth a visit, especially when the sales are on. The best shopping street is Laugavegur, which has a mixture of international names and smaller local retailers. There is an excellent bookshop at No. 18, Mál & Menning, with almost an entire floor given over to titles in English.

The two main shopping centres are Kringlan, on the road of the same name, and the smaller Smáralind on Hagasmára in Kópavogur, just outside Reykjavík. Both are home to many well-known names as well as cafes and restaurants.

For souvenirs try Icelandic woollen sweaters, gloves, scarves and hats. Most are produced by small workshops and come in all shapes, sizes and colours. The Handknitting Association of Iceland's shop at Skólavördustígur 19 has a wide selection. The same street has a number of art galleries selling some excellent local work, as well as craft shops for handicrafts, stones and other minerals. Duvets, quilts and other bedcovers are also high quality, although those filled with locally gathered eider down tend to be expensive.

Smoked salmon, roe caviar and skyr, a tasty Icelandic yoghurt, are good buys, but be aware of the possible import restrictions on food in your own country. Icelandic skin- and healthcare products are making a name for themselves at home and abroad, notably those made at the Blue Lagoon *(see page 65)*; these can be bought in several stores in Reykjavík and at Keflavík airport.

Tax-Free Shopping

On departure from Iceland you can get a refund of the VAT (Value Added Tax) paid on goods over 4,000 Ikr, provided that they were purchased in the previous three months. Ask the shop assistant where you see the 'Tax-Free Shopping' sign, and you will be given a coupon to present at the airport before you leave. If the total is more than 40,000 Ikr, you will have to show the goods themselves on your way out of the country, otherwise just the receipts will do. This scheme can save you about 15 percent on the price of many items.

Chic shoes on Laugavegur

OUTDOOR ACTIVITIES

There can be few capitals in the world better located than Reykjavík for exploring the great outdoors. Hiking, horse-riding, fishing, bird-watching and whale-watching are all possible right on the city's doorstep and all of them can be indulged in, even if your visit to Reykjavík is no longer than a couple of days.

Whale-Watching

Whale-watching started in Iceland as recently as 1995, though curiously it was never possible from Reykjavík at that time. Thankfully, with the increasing popularity of the trips, that has now all changed. Between April and September, tours leave up to three times daily from the main harbour sailing out into Faxaflói bay, where there's a good chance of seeing at least something – the most likely is the common minke whale, although humpbacks, fin and even blue whales are spotted from time to time, as well as dolphins and porpoises. If you don't see anything at all, you will probably be offered a free second trip. Tours are operated by Destination Iceland (*see page 128*). And note that you don't have to be on a boat to see whales – a glance out to sea might reveal a whale's back breaking the surface.

> **Make sure you take plenty of warm clothing and waterproof layers with you on a whale-watching trip, as it tends to be pretty chilly – and choppy – on the sea around Iceland.**

Puffin Tours and Bird-Watching

Reykjavík and its surroundings enjoy a popular following among birdspotters – it is one of the few capitals in Europe where geese and swans regularly overfly the main shopping street. The most accessible place to watch birds is Tjörnin lake, beside the City Hall, right in the heart of the city. Here, you'll be able to spot between 40 and 50 different species of birds, predominantly greylag geese and Whooper swans, although there is also a sizeable colony of Arctic tern towards the lake's southern reaches. Most visitors come to Reykjavík intent on seeing puffins – however, to see these comical birds you'll need to take a boat tour to the tiny island, Akurey *(see page 68)*, which is home to around 30,000 or so of them. Although you can't actually go ashore on the island, the

Whale-watching boats moored in Reykjavík harbour

boat sails close to the cliffs so you'll get a great view of the birds. Tours leave from the main harbour in Reykjavík and last around an hour.

The Icelandic Society for the Protection of Birds can be contacted at PO Box 5069, 125 Reykjavík, <www.birdlife. net/iceland>.

Horse-Riding

There have been horses in Iceland for as long as there have been people in the country. They are used for both farming and riding and can be hired, with or without guides, from several riding centres in the Reykjavík area. You can do treks of

Pure Icelandic horses

various durations, anything from one hour up to a day. If you are bringing your own equipment or clothing it must be disinfected on arrival. One of the most popular establishments for organising horse-riding and treks is the excellent eco-travel company, Íshestar (Sörlaskeiði 26, 220 Hafnarfjörður, tel: 555 7000, <www.ishestar.is>) who run tours of three hours around the local lavafields of Hafnarfjörður or, if you're looking for something more demanding, a day trip to Geysir and Gullfoss on horseback. In Reykjavík itself at Hraunbær 2, another good choice is Thyrill-Víðidalur (tel: 567 3370, <www.islandia.is/thyrill>). The magazine *Eídfaxi International* (<www.eidfaxi.is>) is published for Icelandic horse lovers worldwide.

Walking and Hiking

Undoubtedly the best hiking in the immediate vicinity of Reykjavík is to be had along the Seltjarnarnes-Heidmörk trail, which bisects the capital from northwest to southeast. This well-surfaced trail is easily walked and is suitable for beginners and families. Suggested routes, which vary from one to six hours in duration, are available from the tourist office.

The more ambitious routes around Reykjavík require some previous experience, a high level of fitness and good hiking boots and waterproof clothing. Remember that the Icelandic weather can and does change unexpectedly, and by far the best months for hiking are June, July and August, when the weather is relatively warm, and visibility is at its best.

In fine weather, an excellent hike leads up the steep slopes of Mt Esja, the peak that lies about 10km (6 miles) to the northwest of the capital. At 909m (2,982ft), the summit offers spectacular views not only of Reykjavík but also of Faxaflói bay and up towards the Snæfellsnes Peninsula. Esja is one of the classic destinations around the Icelandic capital, and if hiking is your thing you'll definitely want to include this in your Reykjavík itinerary. The easiest ascent begins beside the Mógilsá river at the Icelandic forestry station building there.

Slightly further afield, though still within easy striking distance of the city, is Hengill, an area of rich vegetation and hot springs criss-crossed by over 100km (60 miles) of hiking trails. It's important to stick to the well laid-out paths here to avoid damaging the highly vulnerable Icelandic flora hereabouts. Walking around Hengill will give you the chance of seeing bubbling mud pools, extensive areas of lava and volcanic craters. Without your

Iceland's isolation and a ban on importing new horses to keep disease at bay means that its horses are very pure. Relatively small but tough, they can handle the country's rugged terrain, are found in a variety of colours and are known for their intelligence, stamina and speed. These horses have a unique gait, a *tölt* – a running walk with a gentle flowing movement.

own transport, you reach Hengill onboard the scheduled bus to and from Selfoss; this leaves from the BSÍ terminal.

Tourist offices can provide bus timetables and maps of all the routes mentioned above, although for advice on safety and protecting the environment the best source of information is the Nature Conservation Agency (Skúlgata 21, 101 Reykjavík, tel: 570 7400, <www.natturuvernd.is>).

Fishing

Salmon fishing in Reykjavík has an international reputation. The season is from around the third week of June until mid-September, though permits need to be obtained well in advance. Contact the National Angling Association (Bolholt 6, 105 Reykjavík, tel: 553 1510, <www.angling.is>). The main salmon river in Reykjavík is the Ellidaár River.

Iceland sits in the North Atlantic's best fishing grounds. Sea angling has traditionally been considered an industry rather than a pastime, but it is now also becoming popular as a sport. The season begins in late May and runs until the end

Water Babies

The swimming pool is to the people of Reykjavík what the pub is to Londoners or the coffeeshop to New Yorkers. It's where people come to meet friends, relax and catch up on the latest gossip, in fact, it's even the place where MPs do much of their campaigning at election time! Although swimming pools across the city are friendly, relaxed places, there's strict etiquette governing their use. Since the level of chlorine in the water is very low, it's compulsory to shower thoroughly, without a swimming costume, before entering the water. Notices posted up in the changing rooms show clearly which parts of your body you need to wash before heading for the pool. Forget, and you're likely to be ticked off and sent back to the showers by the attendants.

Playing in the pool at Laugardalur

of August. Contact Angling Club Lax-á (Vatnsendabletti 181, 203 Kópavogur, tel: 557 6100, <www.lax-a.is>).

Swimming

More than just a sport in Iceland, swimming is a social activity for all the family, and there are geothermally heated pools right across the capital. If you want to do serious lengths, the best pool in Reykjavík is Laugardalslaug on Sunðlaugavegur (tel: 553 4039; open Mon–Fri 5.50am–9.30pm, Sat, Sun 8am–8pm; admission fee). It has a 50-m (165-ft) pool, four hotpots, a Jacuzzi, steam room, sun lamps and waterslide. Other pools include Sunðhöllin (on Barónsstígur), which has a 25m (80-ft) indoor pool and a couple of outdoor hotpots, and Vesturbæjarlaug on Hofsvallagata, in the western part of the capital, also with a 25-m (80-ft) outdoor pool, sauna, hotpots and steam room. Swimming costumes and towels can be hired at all pools for a small fee.

CHILDREN

Reykjavíkers try to involve children in almost all their sporting and cultural activities. Swimming and horse-riding are particularly popular with local children, and families gather in large numbers at weekends to feed the ducks and geese at Tjörnin in front of the City Hall.

The pool at **Laugardalur** *(see page 53)* has a huge 85-m (280-ft) waterslide and a children's pool. At the same site, **Reykjavík's Family Park and Farmyard Zoo** (open daily, summer 10am–6pm, winter Thur–Tues 10am–5pm; admission charge, free for under-fives; *see page 54*) is always a hit with the kids – the seals are fed twice a day (at 11am and 4pm); when they tire of looking at the seals, foxes, reindeer, horses, cows, pigs and all the other animals, they can head for the Family Park. There, they can try their hand at a range of activities, including operating little electric cars, pulling themselves across a man-made lake on a raft, climbing a replica Viking ship, and more. Also in the park, there is a large grill that can be used free of charge for barbecuing.

Enjoying a refreshing drink at the cafe at Öskjuhlíð

For older children there are two **bowling alleys**. The first, Keiluhöllin, is at Öskjuhlíð (open Sun–Tues noon–midnight, Fri, Sat noon–2am; *see page 48*); the second, Keila, is at Mjódd (open Mon–Fri noon–11.30pm, Sat, Sun 10am–11.30pm).

The **Volcano Show** (Hellusund 6a; *see page 40*) is a fascinating film display featuring eruptions, including that of Surtsey island.

Calendar of Events

The precise dates of events change from year to year as they are linked to religious holidays or the seasons. Check with tourist offices for details.

February – Þorrablót. Throughout the month traditional pagan delicacies such as rams' testicles and rotten shark are served up at special Viking feasts as a reminder of times past. Undoubtedly the best place to experience Þorrablót food is at Fjörkráin restaurant in Hafnarfjörður just outside the capital.

3rd Thursday in April – First day of Summer. An optimistic celebration marked with festivities across the city to herald the arrival of lighter days and warmer temperatures.

June 17 – Independence Day. Large and patriotic crowds gather in the centre of the city to celebrate independence from Denmark with street theatre and parades organised in honour of the man who achieved it in 1944, Jón Sigurðsson.

June 24 – Jónsmessa. Reykjavíkers often light bonfires to celebrate Midsummer when, according to folklore, spirits and elves are out in force. By tradition it's also the day to roll naked in the dew to bring good health and fertility.

1st weekend in August – Verslunnarmannahelgi. All shops are closed on this traditional long labour day weekend. Reykjavíkers traditionally head for the countryside where they camp and make merry. The Westman Islands are a particularly popular place to head for.

Late August – Reykjavik Cultural Night. This has become an essential part of cultural life in Iceland with thousands of people strolling the streets of the city on this exciting and eventful night featuring dancing, music and theatre. **Reykjavík marathon**. Held over a distance of 3km (1¾ miles), 5km (3 miles) or 10km (6 miles) around Laugardalur, these timed races draw huge crowds from across the country.

December – Christmas. Although there are no festivities as such to mark the approach of Christmas, it is a magical time to be in Reykjavík when the short, dark days are lit by hundreds of candles in seemingly every window in the city and lights are hung from trees and balconies.

EATING OUT

Going out for a meal in Reykjavík can be a highly variable business – usually, the only thing you can be sure of is that you will feel you have paid a huge amount for what you have just eaten. There is no doubt that the fare served at some of the capital's more upmarket hotels ranks alongside that found in similar establishments elsewhere, but it's worth remembering that the food is aimed primarily at tourists because no Reykjavíker in his or her right mind would dream of paying the ludicrous prices some places charge. Without being overly extravagant, it's easy to clock up 100–120 euros for a three-course dinner with wine in the smarter restaurants about town. If you do want to splurge, it's always a good idea to shop around before actually sitting down to

Outdoor dining at Sólon, on Bankastræti

dine; that way there's a greater chance that your hard-earned money will buy something delicious rather than just something over-priced and overcooked.

Don't think though that you necessarily need to part with vast amounts of cash to fill your stomach in Reykjavík. These upmarket restaurants and tourist traps aside, the growing popularity of the city as a tourist destination over the last few years has led to an explosion in the number of mid-range eating places where it's possible to find something of reasonable quality and not overly expensive.

Surfing the web at one of the city's internet cafes

Meal Times

The best way to get the best value for money when eating out in the Icelandic capital is to follow the example of the city's inhabitants and dine at lunchtime, which in Reykjavík is any time between 11am and 2pm. From Monday to Friday many eateries offer lunch specials, which generally feature a scaled-down version of their evening menu at much reduced prices. Pizzerias and the city's ethnic restaurants are a good first choice at lunchtime and are always busy. Chinese restaurants, for example, generally offer a help-yourself buffet for a set price; although not especially creative, this usually represents good value for money. Evening meals in the city's smarter hotels are generally eaten from 6pm onwards and are more often than not *à la carte* affairs featuring the best of modern Icelandic cuisine. In mid-range restaurants in the city centre you'll find people tend to dine at around 7pm; don't feel under any pressure to vacate your table once you've finished dinner, as it's not common practice in Iceland, unlike in some other countries, to turf guests out once they've finished coffee to make way for the next sitting.

Traditional Foods

The two staple foods are fish and lamb. Fish is plentiful and cheap, so every meal, from breakfast onwards, will usually include it in some form.

The fish you see drying in the wind on racks is haddock or cod used to make *hardfiskur*. It's torn into strips and eaten as a snack, sometimes with butter, with a glass of milk or maybe something stronger.

If you are feeling brave, and think your stomach can take it, search out some *hákarl* – putrified shark meat. It's buried, usually in sand and gravel, for up to six months, which breaks

Food Preservation

The Icelandic capital was effectively cut off from the rest of Europe for centuries, and, with very little in the way of food imports, the art of fine cuisine was late to take hold. The city's population depended on what they could catch or grow themselves, making do with a diet based almost entirely on fish, lamb and vegetables such as potatoes. Various methods were devised to preserve the food so it could be used for months after it was caught. Meat was smoked, salted and pickled. Fish would be hung out and dried, or smoked in dung or salted, or even buried. Today though, Reykjavík food is altogether more sophisticated and cosmopolitan and in this city of barely 110,000 people you can find everything from Indian to Mexican, puffin breast to whale steak.

down the ammonia and toxins in the flesh – there is no mistaking the stench of ammonia when it's dug up again. The shark meat is washed down with a strong liquor known as *brennivín*, which helps to take away some of the taste. The darker meat on the shark, *gler hákarl*, is a little less potent than the white meat, but either way it's an eye-watering experience, to put it very mildly. Occasionally you will find whale meat on the menu; however, as hunting whales for food has been forbidden since 1989, the meat is either from a whale that beached and died or was illegally caught. There is one

Hardfiskur (dried fish), a traditional snack in the making

restaurant in Reykjavík that regularly has whale on the menu if you're tempted – and your conscience will allow it.

Most Icelandic seafood, by contrast, is absolutely delicious and comes to your plate very fresh indeed. Icelandic cod, halibut, turbot and monkfish, for example, are juicy and succulent. Salmon and trout from the rivers are large and relatively inexpensive, as is char, a species of trout that is found across the country. Smoked salmon and gravadlax (sweet marinated salmon) are both of very high quality.

While you will never go short of tasty fish, you might tire of it after a while. The other Icelandic staple, lamb, may cost more, but the taste is exceptional. Sheep farms on the island are small, and the flocks are allowed to graze wild in the highlands, where they eat herbs as well as grass. As a result, the meat has quite a gamey flavour.

As with fish, lamb was traditionally smoked to produce *hangikjöt*, which is eaten hot or cold. Nothing was ever allowed to go to waste in winter in Iceland, and dishes made of sheep's offal are still produced. *Slátur* (literally: slaughter) is a haggis-like dish made from all manner of left-overs, pressed into cakes, pickled in whey and cooked in stomach lining. Alternatively *svid* are boiled-and-singed sheep's heads, minus the

Help-yourself buffet at the Ugly Duckling Restaurant

brains, which are eaten either fresh or pickled. The meat is sometimes then taken off the bone and pressed to produce *svidasulta*. A real delicacy, served on special occasions, is *súrsadir hrútspungar* (pickled rams' testicles).

A limited amount of game finds its way on to the dinner plate. Reindeer from the east of the country is similar to venison. Ptarmigan is a grouse-like bird and a favourite at Christmas time. Icelanders are quite happy to eat their national symbol, too: puffin is often seen on the menu; it is frequently smoked and produces quite a dark, rich meat.

The main locally produced vegetables are potatoes and turnips. Wild berries are often used in sauces and puddings, and rhubarb thrives in the cold climate. Otherwise the dessert course is often cakes or pastries.

Bread, which is often made with rye, is a normal accompaniment to any Icelandic meal. It is sometimes baked in underground ovens in the naturally hot earth to produce *hverabraud* ('steam bread'). Rye pancakes, which are known as *flatkaka*, go particularly well with smoked salmon and other smorgasbord-type toppings.

What to Drink

Not surprisingly, the Icelandic climate is not conducive to wine-growing, so all wines are imported and ruinously expensive. There are high taxes on all alcohol, since – in common with the other Nordic countries – the government tries to discourage alcoholism. It's not that long since beer was actually illegal on the island.

Even today alcohol can only be bought from bars, restaurants and the licensed government liquor stores known as the *vínbúð*. The main outlet in Reykjavík is at Austurstræti 10a and has strictly limited opening times (Mon–Thur 11am–6pm, Fri 11am–7pm, Sat 11am–2pm). The only exception is the very weak beer known as pilsner, which is less than 2.2 percent proof, inexpensive and can be purchased in supermarkets.

Icelandic spirits, on the other hand, are both strong and tasty. *Brennivín* ('burning wine') is a schnapps distilled from potatoes and flavoured with caraway seeds. One brand is known as *Svarti Daudi* or 'Black Death', but don't let that put

The Icelandic term for vegetarian is the cause of many a wry smile among visitors in the know. The pedantic custom of forming names for new concepts from existing words, has created the literal, if rather unflattering, *jurtaæta* or plant eater.

you off. A good variant is Hvannarótar, which is flavoured with angelica.

When they are not drinking alcohol, Icelanders are very keen on coffee, and there are coffee shops everywhere. It's sometimes even offered free from flasks in libraries, shops and supermarkets. Tea is less common than coffee, but is widely available.

To Help you Order

Do you have any vegetarian dishes?	**Eruð þið með grænmetisrétti?**
Is service included?	**Er þjónustugjald innifalið?**
I'd like to pay.	**Ég ætla að borga.**
Can I pay with this credit card?	**Get ég borgað með þessu greiðslukorti?**
Cheers!	**Skál!**

Sushi chef with his minimalist creation

If the Menu isn't in English…

Gætum við/get ég fengið…   Could we/I have…

Basics

ávextir	fruit
bakað	baked
baunir	peas, beans
kartöflur	potatoes
brauð	bread
glóðað	grilled
grænmeti	vegetables
hrísgrjón	rice
kartöflur	potatoes
laukur	onion
ostar	cheeses
reykt	smoked
salat	salad
smjör	butter
súpa	soup
smárettir	snacks
soðið	boiled
steikt	fried

Drinks

appelsínusafi	orange juice
bjór	beer
kaffi	coffee
mjólk	milk
te	tea
vatn	water
vín	wine
(hrauðvín)	(red)
(hvítvín)	(white)

Fiskur (Fish)

bleikja	char
hörpuskel	scallop
humar	lobster
lax	salmon
lúða	halibut
rauðspretta	plaice
sandhverfa	turbot
síld	herring
siltungur	trout
skötuselur	monkfish
steinbítur	catfish
ýsa	haddock
rækja	shrimp
þorskur	cod

Kjöt (Meat)

lambakjöt	lamb
lundi	puffin
nautakjöt	beef
lambakótelettur	lamb chop
nautalundir	beef fillet
nautasteik	beef steak
skinka	ham
kjúklingur	chicken
svínakjöt	pork
lítið steikt	rare
miðlungs steikt	medium
vel steikt	well done

HANDY TRAVEL TIPS

An A–Z Summary of Practical Information

A

ACCOMMODATION

The range of hotel and hostel accommodation in Iceland is very wide indeed. There is a small selection of quality hotels in the capital with character, though these are the exception rather than the rule, and many of the higher-rated hotels are large and impersonal. However, there are plenty of guesthouses in Reykjavík, and these are generally welcoming and considerably cheaper than hotels. They vary in quality, but are invariably clean and well kept. Note, however, that bathrooms are very often shared.

If you are in Reykjavík between May and September you are advised to book ahead, since the number of hotel beds generally falls short of the number of tourists now choosing the Icelandic capital as a destination for a short break or longer holiday.

The Icelandic Tourist Board has recently introduced a classification system for accommodation, but not all hotels have signed up to it. The system grades hotels from four stars, for those with the best facilities, down to one star, for the most basic.

See pages 132–6 for our hotel recommendations.

AIRPORTS

Keflavík:

Reykjavík's international airport (tel: 425 0680) is situated at Keflavík, 55km (35 miles) west of Reykjavík. While it is modern and easy to negotiate, it is certainly not big compared with those of other capital cities. There are Foreign Exchanges both before and after passport control, plus ATMs, which accept most cards. Keflavík is one of the few airports in the world to allow arriving passengers to buy duty-free wine and spirits – all, of course, at lower prices than in hotels and restaurants in the city but still probably more expensive than you're used to paying at home. Car-rental offices are situated in the arrivals hall.

The airport bus into Reykjavík from Keflavík airport costs around 1,100 Ikr and takes 45 minutes. It goes first to the capital's main bus station, from where there are transfers on to most of the bigger hotels.

Taxis from the airport to central Reykjavík will take about half an hour and cost upwards of 8,000 Ikr.

City airport:
Reykjavík's city airport is situated at the opposite end of the runway from the bus station. It is served by all domestic flights as well as international services for the Faroe Islands and Greenland. There are regular buses between downtown Reykjavík and the city airport on route No. 5.

B

BICYCLE HIRE

Tourist offices *(see page 129)* and hotels will have full details of bike rental within Reykjavík. The long-distance bus company, BSÍ (tel: 562 3320, <www.bsi.is>), hires out good-quality mountain bikes and accessories, with discounts if you have one of its bus passes.

BUDGETING FOR YOUR TRIP

Reykjavík is undoubtedly one of the most expensive cities in Europe, but with careful planning the costs can be brought down significantly. The following is intended to give a rough guide to prices only.

Getting to Iceland. Icelandair's long-standing monopoly on flights traditionally meant very high airfares. However, in spring 2003 a new Icelandic budget airline **Iceland Express** (tel: 550 0600, <www.icelandexpress.com>) started operations, with return tickets (including airport taxes) going for around £100 from London Stansted to Keflavík. Although fares have nudged up slightly since then, it's still possible to pick up a return to Reykjavík for just £118 if you book early enough. The cheapest published fares with **Icelandair** (tel: 505 0100) range from £150–280 from London Heathrow and Glasgow to Reykjavík. There are sometimes cheaper so-called 'Lucky Fares' (upwards of £137 from London Heathrow, and £164 from Glasgow) on the Icelandair website <www.icelandair.co.uk>, although there is only limited availability.

If you are flying from the US, Icelandair is still the only option, and you can expect to pay from $600–700 for a return ticket. Check on <www.icelandair.net> for special offers.

Travelling to Iceland by the Faroese-operated **Smyril Line** ferry (<www.smyril-line.fo>) is also expensive. A single ticket with a bed in a four-berth cabin in high season from the Shetland Islands to Seyðisfjördur is currently around €430. You will also incur extra expense travelling by ferry from Aberdeen to Shetland before boarding the Norröna, which then sails via the Faroe Islands en route for Iceland *(see page 117)*.

Accommodation. The more expensive hotels can charge more than 20,000 Ikr a night for a double room in high season, but you can get a good-standard hotel in the city for around 12,000 Ikr. Guesthouses charge around 6,000–7,000 Ikr. In some places you can pay about half the price if you use your own sleeping-bag.

Meals. Dining out costs anything up to 10,000 Ikr a head, without wine, in the best restaurants; wine is extremely expensive regardless of which restaurant you choose, and you will be lucky to find a decent bottle for less than 2,500 Ikr. Dinner in a mid-range hotel might cost 4–5,000 Ikr, again without wine. Check the prices in restaurant windows – you should be able to find a reasonable meal for less than 2,000 Ikr. Lunchtime specials tend to be comparatively good value for money.

Local transport. A Reykjavík bus ticket costs 220 Ikr, but long-distance journeys are expensive by comparison. The **Reykjavík**

Tourist Card *(see page 34)*, available for 24, 48 and 72 hours, entitles you to unlimited travel by bus within Greater Reykjavík (as well as free museum and galllery entrance) for 1,200 Ikr, 1,700 Ikr and 2,200 Ikr respectively. The Card can be bought at venues across the city including the main tourist office.

Bus and coach tours offer good value. At the time of printing, a sightseeing tour of Reykjavík cost 2,900 Ikr per person, and a half-day tour to the nearest waterfalls and geysers was 4,900 Ikr. Whale-watching from Reykjavík costs around 4,000 Ikr. Car hire costs a minimum of 5,000 Ikr per day, with limited mileage, and a full tank of petrol costs approximately 5,500 Ikr.

Taxis. These are relatively expensive. A short journey in town costs about 1,000 Ikr.

Entertainment. Entrance to nightclubs is at least 1,000 Ikr; once inside, beers cost 600 Ikr or more each. A coffee in a standard cafe is around 170 Ikr – more in fashionable drinking holes. A cinema ticket costs in the region of 700 Ikr.

C

CAMPING

Although there are about 125 official campsites throughout Iceland, there's only one in Reykjavík itself, at Sundlaugavegur 34 (tel: 568 6944), to the east of the city centre. Remember if you're planning to leave the capital for a few days and fancy camping within national parks or conservation areas, you're only allowed to put up a tent at designated spots.

A leaflet giving full details of camping in Reykjavík and elsewhere in Iceland is published by the Iceland Tourist Board *(see page 129)*. Equipment can be hired from Sportleigan, Laugavegur 25, Reykjavík, tel: 551 9800, fax: 561 3082.

CAR HIRE *(See also Driving and Budgeting for your Trip)*

Several major international rental companies are represented in Iceland, as well as locally based firms. Prices are high, and insurance, which is compulsory, is not always included in the quoted price, so check first. Note also that you must be at least 20 years old to hire a car in Iceland.

The bigger companies are as follows:

• **Avis**
Tel: 591 4000; <www.avis.com>.

• **Budget**
Tel: 567 8300; <www.budget.com>.

• **Europcar**
Tel: 591 4050; <www.europcar.com>.

• **Hertz**
Tel: 505 0600; <www.hertz.com>.

The best local company is **alp** (tel: 562 6060), located at Dugguvogur 10.

Unmade roads, especially in the interior, require a substantial car, usually a four-wheel drive. Note that insurance does not usually cover you to travel in the interior – check this very carefully before hiring a vehicle.

CLIMATE

Despite its northerly location just south of the Arctic Circle – and the fact that it's the capital of 'Iceland' – Reykjavík isn't actually that cold. The city benefits from the gulf stream and is warmer than much of mainland Scandinavia, for example. However, summers are generally cool, and the city is often wet and windy, with the weather changing dramatically from day to day as well as within the course of one day itself, so it's sensible to be prepared for all eventualities. Unfortunately Iceland's weather generally approaches from the southwest, with the result that heavy rain clouds tend to empty their load on the Icelandic capital first before moving on elsewhere. The weather is drier and sunnier in the north and east, for example, although no less windy. You can get Reykjavík's weather report in English by visiting <www.vedur.is/english>.

The difference between the maximum temperatures recorded in Reykjavík over the year is remarkably small – in July and August the average maximum temperature is barely 14°C (57°F), whereas in December and January it's a respectable 2°C (36°F). The following chart gives the average minimum and maximum temperatures, plus the average rainfall (in millimetres).

	J	F	M	A	M	J	J	A	S	O	N	D
Temperature												
°C min	-2	-2	-1	1	4	7	9	8	6	3	0	-2
°C max	2	3	4	6	10	12	14	14	11	7	4	2
Rainfall												
mm	76	72	82	58	44	50	52	62	66	85	72	79

CLOTHING

Although in summer you may be warm enough in a T-shirt and shorts, it's sensible to pack for bad weather all year round, just in case, with the more layers the better. Waterproof clothing is essential, and if you are planning to spend a lot of time outdoors, invest in windproof outer garments and a good pair of hiking boots (possibly ones that you can attach crampons to, if you are planning on glacier walking). Take plenty of jumpers or fleeces (the latter are good because they dry quickly) to keep you warm plus thick walking socks (and thinner ones to go against your skin). And don't forget to pack a swimming costume, as heated outdoor pools are very much a part of the Icelandic social scene.

Icelanders don't tend to dress up to go out, unless they are going to very expensive restaurants – even there, you wouldn't be expected to wear a tie. Although the younger clubbing crowd is extremely fashion conscious, you shouldn't be turned away from a venue for wearing jeans or trainers.

CRIME AND SAFETY *(See also Emergencies and Police)*

Reykjavík is an extremely peaceful place, and the Icelanders are a law-abiding nation. Public places are well lit, and pickpocketing and street crime are rare, although the city has a number of drug addicts and alcoholics who steal to fund their habits (of the few people in prison, most are drugs offenders), so some caution is always sensible – as it would be anywhere. Drunken crowds of young people in the streets of Reykjavík in the early hours at weekends can be intimidating, but rarely threatening.

CUSTOMS AND ENTRY REQUIREMENTS

Iceland has signed the Schengen Agreement, so, in principle, residents of other Schengen countries (including France, Germany and the US but not Britain and Ireland) can travel without document checks. Flights from the UK arrive at the designated Schengen terminal at Keflavík airport, and passengers are required to go through passport control.

Iceland doesn't require visas from citizens of EU states, the US, Canada, Australia or New Zealand; South African citizens do require one, however. Passports must be valid for at least three months after your arrival date, and visitors may stay for that period. There are no currency restrictions.

D

DRIVING

Despite the high cost of car hire *(see page 109)*, it may provide the only way to see everything you wish in the time available. Driving in Iceland can also be a real pleasure – the roads are not busy and the freedom to stop to admire the scenery or go for a walk is a huge bonus.

Be prepared for journeys to take a lot longer than you might expect from the distances involved, owing to the challenging conditions.

Road conditions. While much of the main highway encircling the country is surfaced, many routes in Iceland are just gravel or unmade and full of potholes. Some roads are prone to flooding, and bridges are often single-lane.

Icelanders drive surprisingly fast, often in the middle of the road, making way for oncoming vehicles at the last minute.

Sandstorms can be a hazard along the coast and in some parts of the interior. In winter, snow and ice are common, and studded snow tyres are essential.

For information on road conditions tel: 1777 between 8am and 4pm or check on <www.vegag.is>.

Rules and regulations. Icelanders drive on the right. The speed limit is 50km/h (30mph) in urban areas, 80km/h (50mph) on gravel roads in rural areas and 90km/h (55mph) on asphalt roads out of the towns.

Driving off roads is illegal, seat belts are compulsory in the front and back of a car, and headlights must be used at all times, day and night. Drink-driving, which is defined as 0.05 percent blood-alcohol content, is taken very seriously by the authorities. Offenders lose their licences and face heavy fines.

Fuel. In Reykjavík most filling stations stay open until 11.30pm. Many have automatic pumps that take credit cards after that time. Around the ring road there are filling stations every 50km (30 miles) or so, but if in doubt fill up before you move on. Prices vary, but it will cost about 5,500 Ikr to fill up the tank of a medium-sized saloon car.

Parking. Reykjavík has plenty of parking meters, ticket machines and car parks, some of which are covered and attended. On-street parking can be hard to find.

Road signs. The usual international symbols are used on road signs.

Akið á eigin ábyrgð	Drive at your own risk
Akið hægt	Drive slowly
Bílastæi	Parking
Blindhæð	Blind summit
Kröpp beygja	Road works
Einbreið brú	Single-lane bridge (often marked by flashing orange lights)
Frost skemmdir	Frost damage
Malarvegur	Dangerous bend
Malbik endar	Unmade road
Þröng brú	Narrow bridge

Help and information. Tourist boards have leaflets about driving on unmade roads and in winter, as well as lists of all road signs. You can also contact Félag Íslenskra Bifreiðaeigenda (Icelandic Automobile Association, or FÍB; tel: 562 9999; <www.fib.is>).

E

ELECTRICITY

The current in Reykjavík is 220 volts, 50 hz ac. Plugs are round pin with two or three prongs. Take an adaptor as necessary

EMBASSIES AND CONSULATES

Australia: Australian citizens should contact the embassy in Copenhagen, Denmark, tel: (+45) 70 26 36 76, fax: 70 26 36 86, <australian.embassy@mail.dks>.
Canada: Túngata 14, 101 Reykjavík, tel: 575 6500, fax: 575 6501, <rkjvk@dfaitomaeci.gc.ca>.
Ireland: Consul General, Ásbúd 106, 210 Gardabær, tel: 554 2355.

South Africa: Hús atvinnulifsins, Borgartún 35, Reykjavík, tel: 591 0355, fax: 591 0358, <jr@mi.is>.
UK: Laufásvegur 31, 101 Reykjavík, tel: 550 5100, fax: 550 5105, <www.britishembassy.is>.
US: Laufásvegur 21, 101 Reykjavík, tel: 562 9100, fax: 562 1020, <www.usa.is>.

The Icelandic Foreign Ministry has a full list of diplomatic representatives abroad on its website: <www.mfa.is>.

EMERGENCIES *(See also Health and Medical Care)*

Police
To contact the police, ambulance or fire service, tel: 112.

Hospitals
For the Emergency Room at Reykjavík City Hospital, tel: 525 1700; outside the capital ask for the nearest Health Centre.

Chemists
Chemists are signed Apótek, and there is at least one in every town. Lyfja at Lágmúli 5 (tel: 533 2300) is open daily 8am–midnight. There's also a branch in the centre of Reykjavík at Laugavegur 16.

Dentists
In case of dental emergencies, tel: 575 0505.

ETIQUETTE

Shyness towards visitors may be mistaken for coldness, but Icelanders are by nature hospitable and innately curious about foreigners and their ways. Family ties are strong yet they are great socialisers, and many a tale is told around the coffee table. In such a small, close-knit society Icelanders invariably find that they are all related, albeit distantly, to one another and are quick to establish connections when introduced, by delving into their family trees.

If you are invited to an Icelander's home, it will most likely be for coffee, often accompanied by copious quantities of cakes and biscuits. The younger generation may be more likely to invite you for dinner; in this case a small gift – wine or flowers, for instance – is appropriate though not essential. It is customary to shake hands, when greeting and leaving, and Icelanders always remove shoes before entering their home.

Smoking is prohibited in public buildings, and the gracious visitor to a private home should always ask for permission before lighting up.

Iceland uses the old system of patronymics, once common throughout Scandinavia. It raises eyebrows when an Icelandic family checks into a hotel abroad – mother, father, son and daughter will all have different last names. Very few Icelanders have surnames. Instead a child takes his father's first name, to which is added son or dóttir (son or daughter) as the case may be. Thus, if a father named Magnús has a son, Jón, and a daughter, Kristín, their full names will be Jón Magnússon and Kristín Magnúsdóttir. And as Icelandic women never change their names on marriage, their mother too will have a different name. A child may also take the mother's name by law, though this is less common. If the identity of the father is not established the child may take the mother's or grandfather's name.

Icelanders always use first names, and visitors will be expected to follow suit. The concept of titles, except for ministers of religion, is unknown. The exception to this is on formal letters when Herra (or Hr.) Magnús Jónsson or Frú Kristín Jensdóttir would be a correct form of address on the envelope.

In the telephone directory, all entries are listed under first names. If the prospect of sifting through pages and pages of Jón Jónsson is daunting, many entries also give the person's profession (in Icelandic) as well as the address.

F

FURTHER READING

• *Angels of the Universe* by Einar Már Guðmundsson, Mare's Nest, London, 1995. This acclaimed novel won the Nordic Council's

Literary Award in 1995. It tells the story of mental disintegration and features a host of colourful characters whose world is at odds with social convention.

• *The Atom Station* by Halldór Laxness, Second Chance Press, New York, 1982. A wonderful dark comedy with a political slant by Iceland's late nobel laureate.

• *Independent People* by Halldór Laxness, Vintage (Random House), USA, 1997. A classic story of a man's struggle for independence, symbolic of the Icelandic nation. The novel won the Nobel Prize.

• *Treasures of Icelandic Verse* by various authors, Mál og Menning, Reykjavík, 1996. An anthology of various Icelandic poems, with both the original and the translation.

• *Troll's Cathedral* by Ólafur Gunnarsson, Mare's Nest, London, 1996. The story of a family beset by violence.

G

GAY AND LESBIAN TRAVELLERS

For its size, Reykjavík has a relatively large and visible gay and lesbian community. The Reykjavík Gay Community Centre, known as Samtökin, is in the centre of town on the fourth floor at Laugavegur 3 (open Mon 8–11pm, Thur until 11.30pm and Sat 10pm–2am; tel: 552 7878, <www.gayiceland.com>). It's a friendly place with a friendly bar, and a book and video library. Other than the Centre there are no exclusively gay bars or clubs in Reykjavík, but Café Cozy at Austurstræti 3 functions as the main meeting place for the gay and lesbian community. Otherwise the bistro and club, 22 at Laugavegur 22 and Jón Forseti, another bar and club at Aðalstræti 10, are both popular. A gay men's leather club runs every Saturday at Bankastræti 11 (from 11pm; tel: 562 1280, <www. this.is/msc>). There is an annual Gay Pride celebration held in Reykjavík every August, <www.this. is/gaypride>. An excellent source of information on the net is also <www.gayice.is>.

GETTING THERE *(See also Airports and Budgeting)*

The fastest and cheapest way to get to Reykjavík is by air. Icelandair flies at least once daily from London Heathrow and four times a week from Glasgow. From London Stansted there is a twice-daily flight with IcelandExpress.

From the US, Icelandair operates from five cities: Baltimore, Boston, Minneapolis, Orlando and New York.

From May to September the Faroese company, Smyril Line <www.smyril-line.fo>, runs a weekly ferry, Norröna, between Hanstholm (Denmark), Tórshavn (Faroe Islands), Bergen (Norway) and Lerwick (Shetland Islands) to Seyðisfjörður in eastern Iceland. Ferry connections for Lerwick are available from Aberdeen. A through journey from London to Iceland using the ferry takes four days, departing on Monday and arriving on Thursday.

H

HEALTH AND MEDICAL CARE *(See also Emergencies)*

Thanks to its clean air and low pollution, Reykjavík is an extremely healthy place. The water is clean to drink, although once you leave the city you should never drink from glacial rivers or streams.

Despite the high latitude, the Icelandic sun can still burn, especially when reflected off snow and ice. Sunblock and good sunglasses should be worn if you are outside for long periods. Windburn can cause chafing of the lips and dehydration, so bring lipsalve with a sunscreen and carry bottles of water with you. Wearing hats and other protection will help, as will a good moisturiser and drinking plenty of fluids.

In extreme circumstances hypothermia is a possibility. It's best avoided by careful planning, wearing layers of warm clothing, taking plenty of rest breaks and eating and drinking sensibly. Symptoms include shivering, numbness, dizzy spells and confused behaviour. If affected, take shelter, remove and replace wet clothing, and consume hot drinks and high-calorie food.

Every year all too mnay visitors are injured, sometimes very seriously, by putting feet or hands into boiling hot mud pools and springs, so take good care to avoid this.

The standard of medical care is very high in Iceland. There is a reciprocal agreement with the UK and Scandinavian countries allowing citizens to receive free health care. However, it doesn't cover prescriptions and some ambulance services. Charges for basic treatment are not particularly high, but good health insurance is still recommended.

If you are planning to take part in any unusual or 'dangerous' sports, make sure that these are covered by your policy. You may have to pay first and reclaim the costs when you get home, so keep all bills and other documentation.

No vaccinations are required to visit Iceland.

L

LANGUAGE

Icelandic is a member of the Germanic language family and is therefore related to English. However, Iceland's isolated location far out in the North Atlantic has caused Icelandic to retain a purity that most other languages in Europe lost long ago. Since the Settlement, speakers of Icelandic only periodically came into contact with native speakers of other tongues with the result that archaic features of medieval Icelandic are still readily used today. Give or take the odd change in pronunciation, the Icelandic spoken in Iceland today is essentially the same tongue spoken by the Vikings more than 1300 years ago.

Although Icelandic is grammatically complex, with four cases and countless declensions to grapple with, anyone who speaks one of the other Scandinavian languages or German will recognise words and structural features. Thankfully, though, there is no need to master Icelandic to enjoy a holiday in Iceland, since nearly all Icelanders speak excellent English. The Icelandic section of the *Berlitz Scandinavian Phrase Book and Dictionary* covers most situations you are likely to encounter. For some of the most important words and phrases, see the box on the page opposite.

Stress, in Icelandic, falls naturally on the first syllable of a word. The following examples of pronunciation are for guidance only – many Icelandic sounds simply do not exist in English.

Vowels and Consonants

a as in hard
á as in how
e as in get
é as in yet
i or **y** as in thin
í or **ý** as in been
o as in ought
ó as in gold
ö as in first
u as in hook
ú as in fool
æ as in fight
au between the sounds in fate and oil, as in the French *feuille*
ey/ei as in day

Ð/ð is th as in the
Þ/þ is th as in thing
fn is pn as in open
g when followed by i (except at the start of a word) is y as in yet
hv is kf as in thankful
j is y as in yet
ll is tl as in bottle
r is always lightly rolled
rl is rtl as in heartless
rn is tn as in button
tn and **fn** when at the end of words are almost silent

Yes	**Já**
No	**Nei**
Hello/hi	**Halló/hæ**
Good morning/afternoon	**Góðan dáginn**
Good evening	**Gott kvöld**
Good night	**Góða nótt**
Goodbye	**Bless**
How do you do?	**Sæll (to a man); sæl (to a woman)**
Fine, thanks	**Mél liður vel, takk**
Thank you	**Takk fyrir**
Yesterday/today/tomorrow	**Í gær/í dag/á morgun**
Where/when/how?	**Hvar/hvenær/hvernig?**
How long/how far	**Hvað lengi/hversu langt**
Left/right	**Vinstri/hægri**
Hot/cold	**Heitt/kalt**
Old/new	**Gamalt/ungt**
Open/closed	**Opið/lokað**
Vacant/occupied	**Laus/upptekinn**

LOST PROPERTY

For lost property, contact the police station at Borgartún 33, Reykjavík, tel: 569 9018 (open Mon–Fri 10am–noon and 2pm–4pm).

M

MAPS

It is not essential to buy a map before arriving in Reykjavík. If you're content to explore the central areas of the city, a combination of the maps in this book and those provided free by the tourist office should be more than adequate. However, if you wish to explore a little wider, getting hold of a detailed map of Iceland is a good idea, and there are a large number available.

The best maps are those produced by the Icelandic National Land Survey, Landmælingar Íslands. This company publishes a 1:500,000 road map of the whole country and also a series of nine 1:250,000 sheets for all regions – these regional maps should be detailed enough for hiking. Less detailed are those produced by Mál og Menning in its Íslandkort series. These are widely available in shops and at filling stations. Mál og Menning also publishes a series of geological maps, which are entitled Náttúrufarskort.

MEDIA

English-language newspapers and magazines are on sale in Reykjavík, usually several days after publication in their home country. They can also be found in public libraries. Local papers and magazines are almost all in Icelandic, although there is a daily news-sheet, *Icelandic Review* (<www.icenews.is>), which is available at some newsagents and hotels. Two magazines, *Iceland Review* (<www.icelandreview.com>) and *Icelandic Geographic* (<www. icelandgeographic.is>) are published in English; both publications are notable for their informative articles and magnificent photography. The main national newspaper, *Morgunblaðið*, has daily news in English on its website <www.mbl.is>.

Many hotels have satellite television, with English and American channels, and you'll find a summary of English-language news on Teletext page 130 of the Icelandic national broadcaster, Sjónvarpid. For world news on the radio try BBC World Service on FM 90.9.

MONEY *(see also Budgeting for your Trip)*

The Icelandic currency is the króna, usually abbreviated to Ikr. Banknotes come in 500, 1,000, 2,000 and 5,000 Ikr denominations, and there are 100, 50, 10, 5 and 1 Ikr coins.

Currency exchange. Foreign exchange is available at all three chains of the Icelandic banks: Íslandsbanki, Landsbanki Ísland and Búna›arbanki, which charge a nominal commission or sometimes nothing at all. Banks open from 9.15am–4pm and offer the best rates of exchange. Out of banking hours you can exchange money at major hotels or the Change Group, which has branches in Reykjavík and stays open late. Banks and the Change Group can also arrange International Money Transfers.

At the time of going to press, the rate of exchange was as follows: £1 = 116 Ikr; E1 = 82.5 Ikr; $1 = 71 Ikr.

Credit cards. Credit cards, in particular Visa and MasterCard, are accepted almost everywhere, although guesthouses may take cash only. Íslandsbanki also accepts Diners Club. Banks and some larger post offices give cash advances against credit cards. American Express customers are advised to call (+44) 1273 571600 to find out where their card will be accepted.

ATMs. There are cash machines at Keflavík airport and at many banks. This is often the cheapest way of getting money, if your card is part of the international Visa, Cirrus, Maestro and Electron networks. The charges will depend on your bank, but the exchange rate is generally better than any other metho of money exchange.

Travellers cheques. These are still accepted, although fewer people carry them than in previous years, due to the popularity and convenience of taking money out at ATMs. To cash travellers cheques, you need also to show your passport.

OPENING HOURS

Shops, banks and other services rarely close for lunch. In general their opening hours are as follows:

Banks: 9.15am–4pm
Post offices: 8.30am–4.30pm

Shops: Mon–Sat 9am–6pm. Smaller shops may not open until 10am.
Supermarkets: open Sun 10am–2 or 6pm.
Liquor Stores: Mon–Thur 11am–6pm, Fri 11am–7pm, Sat 11am–2pm.

P

PHOTOGRAPHY

Crystal-clear air and long hours of daylight create ideal conditions for photography, and enthusiasts may go through more film than they plan to. Note that you should always use a UV/skylight filter when photographing outdoors. All photographic equipment, film and processing is very expensive (think of a number and double it), so bring your own or purchase it at the Duty Free Shop at the Keflavík airport. If you do have to buy film in Iceland, bear in mind that outside Reykjavík slide film, in particular, may be hard to obtain.

POLICE

In such a law-abiding country the police *(lögregla)* keep a low profile, and you are unlikely to come across them unless you commit a motoring offence. They can normally speak some English.

Police Emergency Number, tel: 112.

Reykjavík Police Headquarters is at Hverfisgata 113–115, tel: 569 9020. The city-centre police station is at Tryggvagata 19, tel: 569 9025.

For lost property, contact the police station at Borgartún 33, Reykjavík, tel: 569 9018 (open Mon–Fri 10am–noon and 2pm–4pm).

POST OFFICES

The Icelandic postal service is efficient, and the main post office (open Mon–Fri 9am–4.30pm) in Reykjavík is centrally located at Pósthússtræti 5. The office at Grensásvegur 9, Reykjavík is also open on Saturday, 10am–2pm.

It takes up to five days for post to reach Europe or North America and 10 days for Australia, New Zealand and South Africa.

All post offices offer international express mail, TNT and poste restante facilities. If you are receiving mail, ensure that the sender underlines your surname or writes it in capital letters, as Icelanders sort mail by the first name.

At the time of publication, a first-class *(A-póstur)* letter weighing less than 20g (0.7oz) costs 65 Ikr to Europe and 90 Ikr to the rest of the world. The prices for a first-class letter between 21g and 50g (1.75oz) are 120 Ikr and 165 Ikr. There are up-to-date prices and information at <www.postur.is>.

PUBLIC HOLIDAYS

The following are public holidays in Iceland. Note that most businesses, banks and shops will be closed on these days, and public transport will be more limited than usual. For more information on Icelandic festivals, *see page 95*.

1 January	New Year's Day
1 May	Labour Day
17 June	National Day
24 December	Christmas Eve (from noon)
25 December	Christmas Day
26 December	Boxing Day
31 December	New Year's Eve (from noon)

Moveable dates:
Maundy Thursday
Good Friday
Easter Sunday
Easter Monday
First day of summer
Ascension Day
Whit Sunday
Whit Monday
Bank Holiday Monday (first Monday in August)

PUBLIC TRANSPORT

Buses. There is an excellent bus system both in Reykjavík and across the country. In the capital there are two terminals for the orange city buses: one near the harbour at Lækjartorg, at the junction of Lækjargata and Austurstræti, and the other at Hlemmur and the far end of the main shopping street, Laugavegur. Maps showing all the routes are available from terminals and tourist offices. Services run Mon–Fri, 7am–midnight, and Sun 10am–midnight. There is a flat fare of 220 Ikr, which must be paid in exact change as you board.

If you are changing buses ask for a *skiftimidi,* which is valid on all buses for 45 minutes. A strip of nine tickets, a *farmidaspjald,* costs 1,500 Ikr. A 30-day Green Card, offering unlimited travel, costs 4,500 Ikr. Children under six years old travel free, and there are reduced fares for under 18 year olds.

Long-distance buses operate from the BSÍ Coach Terminal, Vatnsmyrarvegur (tel: 591 1020, <www.bsi.is>). There is a variety of passes available if you are going to use the bus network extensively. The Full-Circle Passport allows you to travel once round the country in either direction, stopping as often as you like. The Omnibus Passport allows unrestricted travel for between one and four weeks.

Taxis. Taxis are available across Reykjavík and cost about 1,000 Ikr for 3km (2 miles). Although taxis are not hailed in the street in Reykjavík as in many other cities, there are ranks on Lækjargata and Eiríksgata. To order a cab by phone call:
• Borgarbill, tel: 552 2440
• BSR, tel: 561 0000
• Hreyfill, tel: 588 5522
   Taxis offer sight-seeing tours at around 3,500 Ikr an hour.

Flights. Air Iceland is the domestic carrier, running flights to the larger towns throughout the country (tel: 570 3030, <www.airiceland.is>) as well as to the Westman Islands. An Air Iceland Pass with four, five or six sectors valid for 30 days, and a Fly As You Please Pass, allowing 12 days' unlimited travel on domestic flights, can only be purchased before you enter Iceland.

Ferries. Herjólfur is the ferry linking Þórlákshöfn to the Westman Islands (tel: 481 2800, <www.herjolfur.is>). Seatours/Smidjustígur 3 (tel: 438 1450, <www.saeferdir.is>) runs ferries to Flatey and Brjánslækur in the West Fjords, as well as operating fjord trips and other excursions.

Train Travel. There are no trains on Iceland.

R

RELIGION

Iceland has been Christian for more than 1,000 years. Ninety percent of the population adhere to the National Church of Iceland, which is evangelical Lutheran, and there are churches and chapels all over the country, even on some farms. About 1 percent of the population is Roman Catholic.

Reykjavík has two cathedrals and the imposing Hallgrímskirkja. Dómkirkjan, the Protestant cathedral (Austurvöllur, tel: 551 2113), holds communion services on Sunday at 11am. At Kathólska Kirkjan, the Catholic cathedral (Túngata, tel: 552 5388), Mass is celebrated in English on Sunday at 6pm. At Hallgrímskirkja (Skólavörduholt, tel: 510 1000), Sunday Mass is held at 11am.

S

SMOKING

Smoking is banned in public places in Iceland.

SPAS

See page 65 (on the Blue Lagoon) and pages 92 and 93, on swimming.

T

TELEPHONES

The code for Iceland is +354, followed by a seven-digit number. There is no area code for Reykjavík or any other town or city throughout the country. To call abroad from Iceland, dial 00, plus the country code. If you use the Iceland telephone book, remember that it lists people by their first names.

Useful numbers
114: international directories
115: international operator
118: directories assistance

Payphones are found in post offices, filling (petrol) stations and on the street. These take coins or phone cards, which can be bought at post offices in various denominations. There are three mobile-phone operators providing GSM and NMT services, with the latter covering more of the country than the former. Pre-paid cards can be bought at filling stations.

TIME DIFFERENCES

Iceland is on GMT all year round. Time in summer is as shown in the box below.

Los Angeles	Chicago	New York	**Iceland**	London	Sydney
5am	7am	8am	**noon**	1pm	10pm

TIPPING

Service is always included in the bill, so tipping is not normally required. It is not usual to tip taxi drivers.

TOILETS

Reykjavík has an excellent plumbing system, and toilets are almost always clean and well maintained. There are toilets in restaurants, cafes and bars for customers, but public toilets are few and far between – there is only one in Reykjavík, close to the tourist office at the junction of Bankastræti and Lækjargata.

TOURS *(See also Public Transport)*

One of the best ways of seeing the main sites around Reykjavík is by organised coach tour. The drivers and tour leaders are always well informed and speak English. If you want to travel into the interior or on to glaciers, a tour is often the only choice. Tours are well run, and many allow you to do some exploring by yourself. The main operators are **Reykjavík Excursions** tel: 562 1011, <www.re.is> and **Destination Iceland**, tel: 591 1020, <www.dice.is>. As well as sightseeing tours of the Geysir geyser, Gullfoss waterfall and Þingvellir parliament site (known as the Golden Circle tour – *see pages 59–65*) there are also whale- and bird-watching tours. Day tours also include the Blue Lagoon, the Snæfellsnes peninsula, Landmannalaugar geothermal area, the Westman Islands and the northern city of Akureyri.

With several days in the city at your disposal, it's worth considering devoting one of them to a glacier tour by snowmobile – a safe, fun (though quite expensive) way to see some of Europe's biggest icecaps close up. The best take you on to the Vatnajökull glacier in southeast Iceland and the Langjökull glacier in the west near Húsafell. Contact **Icelandic Adventure** (Tangarhöfði 7, 112 Reykjavík, tel: 577 5500, <www.adventure.is>) or Destination Iceland at the BSÍ bus terminal on Vatnsmyrarvegur in Reykjavík (tel: 591 1020, <www.dice.is>).

Note that many tours do not operate in 'winter' (generally September to May). For full details, contact the Icelandic Tourist Office *(see opposite)* or look on their website, <www.icetourist.is>, where there is a list of authorised operators and travel agencies.

TOURIST INFORMATION

The tourist information structure in Iceland is a little complex. The Icelandic Tourist Board (Lækjargata 3, Reykjavík, tel: 535 5500, <www.icetourist.is>), promotes Iceland abroad. The regional Tourist Information Centres are separately run, and some parts of the country also have Marketing Agencies. All the various offices offer more information than you could possibly need. Staff speak excellent English and are usually very helpful. Opening times vary, but in summer they open early and close around 7pm.

The Tourist Information Centre in Reykjavík is at Aðalstræti 2, tel: 562 3045, <www.visitreykjavik.is> and <www.icetourist.is> (open daily June–Aug 8.30am–6pm, Sept–May Mon–Fri 9am–5pm, Sat, Sun 10am–2pm).

In the US, contact the Icelandic Tourist Office, 655 Third Avenue, New York, NY 10017, tel: 212 885 9700, <www.icelandtourist-board.com>.

While there are no Icelandic Tourist Offices in Australia, Canada, Ireland, New Zealand or South Africa, in the UK Icelandair at 172 Tottenham Court Road, London, W1P 9LG, can provide a fair amount of brochures and leaflets. Elsewhere information can be obtained worldwide from the excellent <www.icetourist.is>.

Hvar er ferðaskrifstoftan?	Where is the tourist office?
Hvar er/eru…?	Where is/are the…?
strönd	beach
grasagarðurinn	botanical gardens
dómkirkja	cathedral
miðbær	city centre
sýning	exhibition
höbn	harbour
safn	museum
verslanir	shops

TRAVELLERS WITH DISABILITIES

Wheelchair access is available at most of the major hotels. The rough terrain and the lack of developed facilities mean wheelchair access to Iceland's natural wonders is rare. There are paved paths at Geysir, Gulfoss and Þingvellir National Park. For information on vehicles for hire suitable for disabled persons, contact one of the tour operators or tourist information offices. Highland buses for wheelchair users are available on request.

The Icelandic Hotel and Restaurant Association publishes a leaflet entitled *Hotels and Guesthouses*, which lists establishments that are accessible to the disabled. Larger department stores in Reykjavík, as well as the Kringlan Mall, are accessible to wheelchair users. The ferries Baldur and Herjólfur also have good facilities for the disabled. All airlines flying to and from the country can accommodate disabled passengers.

Sjálfsbjörg, the Association of the Disabled in the Capital Area, has published an English-language booklet entitled *Accessible Reykjavík*, which lists establishments and institutions accessible to the disabled.

W

WEBSITES AND INTERNET CAFES

Websites

Every business and organisation in Reykjavík, large and small, now seems to have a website. In addition to those listed in the sections above, the following provide useful information before you arrive in Iceland:
• <www.visitreykjavik.is> (official tourist information site for Reykjavík)
• <www.eyeoniceland.com> (information, photographs, books and listings with useful links to specialist sites)
• <www.natturuvernd.is> (Nature Conservation Agency site with valuable information on safety and protecting the environment)
• <www.this.is/iceland> (tours, excursions, weather, etc)
• <www.whatson.is> (details of events)

- <www.bluelagoon.is> (information on the Blue Lagoon)
- <www.netidinfo.com> (information on what's on in Reykjavík)
- <www.norvol.hi.is> (volcanoes in Iceland)
- <www.nn.is> (Icelandic telephone numbers)
- <www.icelandreview.com> (news about Iceland)
- <www.ruv.is> (Icelandic national radio and television)
- <www.airport.is> (flight information for Keflavík airport)

Internet Cafes

The cheapest way to get on to the internet in Reykjavík is at public libraries, where access is free, although you may have to wait to get to a terminal. Internet cafes are springing up around the country, and costs vary – for instance, in some you pay for access, but the coffee is free.

WEIGHTS AND MEASURES

The metric system is used in Iceland.

Y

YOUTH HOSTELS

The Icelandic Youth Hostel Association (<www.hostel.is>) has 26 excellent hostels from which to choose, including a Reykjavík one at Sundlaugavegur 34, 105 Reykjavík (tel: 553 8110, fax: 588 9201; email: <info@ hostel.is>), 3km (1¾ miles) east of the city centre at the edge of Laugardalur Park (10-minute journey on the No. 5 bus, or a 30-minute walk). The Rekjavík hostel is inordinately popular and fills up quickly in summer when it is essential to book ahead (you can do this via the web). The association can provide a booklet listing hostels and the facilities they offer – most hostels have two- to six-bed rooms and family rooms. You can use your own sleeping-bag/linen or hire what you need. Good deals on car hire and excursions are also offered by the association.

Recommended Hotels

The quality of the accommodation offered by Reykjavík's hotels is unfailingly high, though sadly, so too is the price. Although hotel rooms are never short of creature comforts – they always come with television, telephone and more often than not minibar – their decor can be rather anodyne. Hotels that go in for style in a big way are pointed out in this guide, otherwise you're looking at perfectly comfortable rooms, usually with wooden flooring and chrome fittings. An eat-as-much-as-you-want breakfast buffet, entitling you to return to the table as many times as you wish, is usually included in the room rate.

Guesthouses in Reykjavík represent much better value for money than the city's hotels, though their rooms are naturally not as well-appointed. There is often little to choose between guesthouses, so should you opt to stay in one, make location your deciding factor. Breakfast is sometimes included in the room rate, though if not, it generally costs around 800–900 lkr extra. During the summer (essentially June to August, inclusive), it's worth making an advance booking, since the recent influx of tourists into the city has left hotels and guesthouses struggling to cope.

The price guidelines below are for a double room with bathroom in high season, including breakfast and tax, unless otherwise stated. Most hotels accept major credit cards.

€€€€€	over 250 euros
€€€€	200–250 euros
€€€	160–200 euros
€€	120–160 euros
€	90–120 euros

REYKJAVÍK

Álfhóll Guesthouse € *Ránargata 8, tel: 898 1838, fax: 552 3838, <www.islandia.is/alf>.* A cosy little guesthouse located a short distance from the centre, with clean, comfortable rooms and shared bathrooms. The name means 'Elves' House', and the owners are always more than happy to tell you all you need to know about Iceland's trolls.

Hótel Borg €€€€ *Pósthússtræti 11, tel: 551 1440, fax: 551 1420,* *<www.hotelborg.is>*. No expense has been spared in decorating the rooms in this imposing art deco building close to the Parliament and overlooking Austurvöllur. Oozing character, with period furnishings, this is *the* most exclusive hotel in Reykjavík and accordingly popular with visiting dignitaries. Definitely worth considering if you're in the capital for a special occasion and want some indulgence.

Hótel Cabin €€€ *Borgartún 32, tel: 511 6030, fax: 511 6031,* *<www.keyhotel.is>*. Hótel Cabin is located a little out of the centre but still within a 15-minute walk of the main shopping area. This large hotel has terrific views out over Faxaflói bay and the mountains beyond. Unusually, the owners promote rooms that face into the corridor, aiming at those who find the all-night summer sunshine keeps them awake. Brightly furnished, well-equipped rooms.

Frón €€€ *Klapparstígur 35a, tel: 511 4666, fax: 522 2790,* *<www.hotelfron.is>*. An absolute find if you're looking for upmarket self-catering hotel accommodation. In terms of location, too, a stone's throw off the main shopping street, Laugavegur, this modern and comfortable hotel is hard to beat. Studios and apartments are available each with their own bathroom and kitchenette. Breakfast is also available should you choose not to go entirely self-catering.

Hótel Holt €€€€€ *Bergstaðastræti 37, tel: 552 5700, fax: 562 3025, <www.holt.is>*. Part of the Relais and Châteaux chain, this hotel is very elegant and comfortable, with great character and style. The public areas are an art-lover's delight, with the largest private collection of Icelandic paintings in existence. The rooms are well equipped, if a little small, and the restaurant is superb. A very special place, but at a price – and breakfast is extra.

Ísafold €€ *Bárugata 11, tel: 561 2294; <www.randburg.com>*. Located in a quiet residential street barely a 10-minute walk from the city centre, this friendly guesthouse is one of the city's best in terms of both quality and price. Although rooms (some of them are a little on the cramped side) share facilities, they are decorated with stylish art and wonderful old-fashioned furniture.

Jörd € *Skólavördustígur 13a, tel: 562 1739, fax: 562 1735.* Cheap and cheerful and right in the centre of town, this guesthouse may lack style and charm but it's a good deal for the location just round the corner from the main shopping street, Laugavegur. Breakfast is extra.

Hótel Klöpp €€€€ *Klapparstígur 26, tel: 511 6062, fax: 511 6071, <www.centerhotels.is>.* Located right in the centre of town, this hotel has a cool, minimalist style, with lots of slate, wooden decor, large windows and brightly decorated bedrooms. The breakfast room is open all day for light snacks, but there is no restaurant. It's hard to beat this hotel in terms of quality, price and location.

Kríunes Guesthouse €€ *Lake Elliðaárvatn, tel: 567 2245, fax: 567 2226, <www.kriunes.is>.* The delightful setting beside the lake makes the short taxi drive out of the city to this tastefully converted former farmhouse worthwhile. Unusual Hispanic decor. Kitchen facilities are available to guests.

Hotel Leifur Eríksson €€€ *Skólavörðustígur 45, tel: 562 0800, fax: 562 0804, <www.hotelleifur.is>.* Set right beneath the Hall-grímskirkja church, this is a friendly family-run place. It has basic but comfortable rooms and a snack bar serving light meals and drinks 24 hours a day.

Hotel Loftleiðir €€€€ *City Airport, tel: 444 4500, fax: 444 4501, <www.icehotel.is>.* This Icelandair-owned hotel is desperately in need of a makeover, with its tired rooms and public areas more reminiscent of pre-revolution Eastern Europe than style-conscious Scandinavia. Sadly, many people on Icelandair packages end up here and leave Reykjavík disappointed with their accommodation. The hotel is large, unfriendly and a good 30-minute walk to the city centre. However, unlike other hotels, it does have its own (small) pool and sauna.

Luna Guesthouse €€€ *Spítalastígur 1, tel: 511 2800, fax: 511 2801, <www.luna.is>.* This place is a cut above the average guesthouse. It's an old family home, converted to provide a handful of elegant two-room apartments and studios, each with a bathroom and a sofa-bed in the living room.

Nordica €€€€€ *Suðurlandsbraut 2, tel: 444 5000, fax: 444 5001,* *<www.icehotel.is>*. This recently renovated hotel (formerly the Esja), the largest in Iceland, is oversized and impersonal. True, this place is the last word in Nordic design with its glass and chrome interiors, yet it has a cold feel to it. Rooms at the front look out over Faxaflói bay and offer hard-to-match vistas. A walk into town from the Nordica will take you at least 25 minutes.

Óðinsvé €€€€ *Þórsgata 1, tel: 511 6200, fax: 511 6201, <www. hotelodinsve.is>*. The pleasant, relaxed atmosphere and stylish but subtle decoration make this hotel, in a quiet residential quarter close to the centre, a comfortable place to stay. There are internet connections, a trouser press and hair dryer in every room. The restaurant is run by a well-known Icelandic celebrity chef.

Plaza €€€€ *Aðalstræti 4, tel: 590 1400, fax: 590 1401, <www.icelandhotels.is>*. This recently-opened hotel is a delightful mix of old and new: heavy wooden beams line the ceilings, and solid wooden floors and white walls add a touch of contemporary Scandinavian style. It's in an enviable location close to some of the city's best bars and clubs and a 2-minute walk away from the Parliament and Austurvöllur. If you're looking for style at more reasonable rates than the Borg or Holt, this is a good bet.

Radisson SAS **Saga €€€€€** *Hagatorg, tel: 525 9900, fax: 525 9909, <www.radissonsas.com>*. A Radisson-SAS hotel, with the usual business and leisure facilities and functional rooms of establishments in that group. There are great views over the city from the skyline restaurant plus a geothermally heated pool on the roof.

Room with a View €–€€€ *Laugavegur 18, tel/fax: 552 7262, <www. roomwithaview.is>*. For a good, cost-effective alternative to a hotel, try these pleasant sixth-floor apartments above the main shopping street. A kitchen and steambath are available to guests, and the balconies offer impressive views. Gay friendly.

Hotel Skjaldbreið €€€€ *Laugavegur 16, tel: 511 6060, fax: 511 6070, <www.centerhotels.is>*. On the main shopping street, this is the partner to the Hótel Klöpp, which is just round the corner. It's the less welcoming of the two, although the rooms are similar and the style is equally trendy.

Travel Inn € *Sóleyjargata 31, tel: 561 3553, fax: 561 3993, <www.dalfoss.is>*. With good views out over Tjörnin lake and barely a 10-minute walk from central Reykjavík, this guesthouse is one of the city's best. It has good-sized rooms and friendly, personable staff.

EXCURSIONS

Hótel Geysir € *Haukadal Biskupstungum, 801 Selfoss, tel: 480 6800, fax: 480 6801, <www.geysircenter.com>*. Located right next to the world-famous geysers, the area's former sports academy has been converted into a modern, very pleasant place to stay. It's a friendly, family-run establishment and gets very busy with tour groups in high season. There are hot tubs (accessible in summer only) and an outdoor pool.

Hótel Klaustur €€€ *Klausturvegur 6, Kirkjubæjarklaustur, tel: 487 4900, fax: 487 4614, <www.icehotel.is/klaustur>*. Icelandair has built this large modern hotel in a town with literally one street, but it's very welcome as there is nothing else of this standard for some distance around. Out of season you could even find you have the whole place to yourself. The friendly and helpful staff are always welcoming.

Hótel Þórshamar €€ *Vestmannabraut 28, Heimaey, Westman Islands, tel: 481 2900, fax: 481 1696, <www.hotel.eyjar.is>*. This is the only hotel in Heimaey (guesthouses are the norm on the island). There are videos and radios in the rooms in the main building – useful when the weather closes in – although not in their second, more basic, building down by the harbour.

Hreiðrið Guesthouse € *Faxastígur, Heimaey, Westman Islands, tel: 481 1045, fax: 481 1414*. A popular alternative to the only hotel on Heimaey and very good value. Staying here feels like being taken into an Icelander's home.

Recommended Restaurants

Surprisingly for a city the modest size of Reykjavík, there is a plethora of restaurants and cafes serving up a whole range of different dishes. You'll find most of them either on or around the main shopping street, Laugavegur, although there are also a couple clustered around the parallel streets to the north of Austurvöllur. In Reykjavík there is often a fine distinction between a bar/cafe and a restaurant, with some establishements functioning primarily as a cafe or a bar during the day and then mutating into a restaurant in the evening. Portions are more often than not on the generous side, so if you're looking to cut costs a little, missing out on a starter is unlikely to leave you hungry but will make a big difference to the bill; although starters are always less expensive than a main course, you'll find sometimes that the difference in price is barely the equivalent of 3–5 euros. Remember, too, that opting for a bottle of wine over dinner will add the equivalent of at least 60 euros to the bill.

The prices indicated below, given as guides only, are for a starter, main course and dessert, but not wine, per person. Tax and service are always included in the bill, but if you wish you can leave a little more for exceptional service. Most restaurants accept major credit cards.

€€€€	over 10,000 lkr
€€€	5,000–10,000 lkr
€€	2,500–5,000 lkr
€	below 2,500 lkr

REYKJAVIK

Apótek €€€ *Austurstræti 16, tel: 575 7900*. This is the kind of place where you will spot Reykjavík's young, fashionable folk, who don't mind paying a bit over the odds. It's very trendy, with low lighting and soft music, and gets pretty lively at weekends. Located on the site of a former chemist – hence the name – Apótek is still a little clinical for some tastes. However, the food, especially the fish-based starters, is consistently good, and the menus are changed on a regular basis to keep people coming back for more.

Hótel Borg €€€€ *Pósthússtræti 11, tel: 551 1440*. Eat here in art deco splendour and imagine that you are back in the 1930s – except, of course, for the distinctly 21st-century prices. The menu is eclectic and includes delights such as slow-cooked pigeon with exotic fruits, and duck-liver paté.

Café Paris €€ *Bergstaðastræti 37, tel: 551 1020*. A Reykjavík classic, this cosy little cafe in the corner of Austurvöllur has been here as long as anyone can remember and outdates its more modern rivals by years. Quintessentially Parisian in style and feel – though with much friendlier waiters – this is a good choice for a light lunch and a good cup of coffee.

Caruso € *Þingholtsstræti 1, tel: 562 7335*. A cosy Italian bistro on three floors in the centre of town, doing good pizzas and pasta dishes and healthy salads. Very welcoming with no pretensions.

Eldsmiðjan € *Bragagata 38a, tel: 562 3838*. If you're craving a traditional Italian pizza, look no futher than Eldsmidjan, literally the 'fire smithy', where they cook top-quality thin-based pizzas in a wood-burning oven. This place is inordinately popular with Reykjavíkers, and there's often a queue to get a table. It's definitely worth the wait, though.

Grænn Kostur € *Skólavörðustígur 8, tel: 552 2028*. A great little vegetarian restaurant with good-value, wholesome food. There is a choice between two main courses of the day, although you can have a little of each, and the menu changes daily. The famed garlic and chilli sauce is always available, however, and people come from far and wide to taste it. Delicious banana, apple and carrot cakes to finish off the meal.

Hornið €€ *Hafnarstræti 4, tel: 551 3340*. Although Reykjavík restaurants come and go at an alarming pace, this Italian-inspired place has stood the test of time and is deservedly popular with the locals. Serving everything from pizzas and pasta to delicious fish dishes, this is a good choice for an informal and relaxed dinner at moderate prices.

Hótel Holt €€€€ *Bergstaðastræti 37, tel: 552 5700.* Arguably the best restaurant in the capital with a magnificent, if rather dark, dining room full of Icelandic art. The chef uses fresh local produce, including a wide range of fish, reindeer and lamb, and presents the dishes with creativity. The bill will be as eye-watering as the food is mouth-watering, but you won't be disappointed.

Jómfrúin € *Lækjargata 4, tel: 551 0100.* Somewhat expensive Danish open sandwiches on rye or French bread, although there's a huge range of toppings (around 150 of them), from crispy bacon and liver pâté to caviar and eggs. Good for a healthy lunch option close to Tjörnin lake.

Lækjarbrekka €€€ *Bankastræti 2, tel: 551 4430.* This is Icelandic cuisine at its very best in one of the oldest buildings (dating from 1835) in Reykjavík. There's a romantic dining room downstairs and a more modern one above. The vast menu has more than 40 dishes, mostly featuring Icelandic seafood and lamb. The lobster is superb, and the delicious home-baked puddings are definitely worth leaving space for.

Metz €€–€€€ *Austurstræti 9, tel: 561 3000.* Although people do come to this upmarket brasserie for the tasty lunches, ranging from salads and quiches to various seafood dishes, it's equally well renowned for its fancy decor. The hand of Britain's style guru, Sir Terence Conran, can still be seen on the interior fittings – just make sure you're wearing your sharpest outfit to match.

Póstbarinn € *Pósthússtræti 13, tel: 562 7830.* An unpretentious cafe/restaurant serving filling sandwiches, soups, fried fish and other snacks for around 1,000 Ikr, making it one of the best lunchtime bargains in the city – plus there are good views of Austurvöllur and the Parliament from its large windows.

Primavera €€–€€€ *Austurstræti 9, tel: 561 8555.* Come here for top-class Italian cooking with sun-dried tomatoes, puréed mushrooms and balsamic vinegar featuring strongly on the menu. There's a large, minimalist dining room on the first floor, where even the slightly brusque service is reminiscent of Italy. The menu isn't extensive, but the quality is uniformly good, and the chocolate puddings are to die for.

Rossopomodoro €€ *Laugavegur 40a, tel: 561 0500.* The latest Italian restaurant to open in Reykjavík and definitely worth a look. With an emphasis on fresh ingredients, the pizzas and pasta dishes here are all reasonably priced and made to order – the open kitchen gives diners a chance to watch the chefs at work. A warm welcome and fast becoming one of the mainstays of authentic Italian cuisine in the Icelandic capital.

Siggi Hall €€€ *Óðinstorg, tel: 511 6200.* Run by and named after Iceland's most well-known celebrity chef, this place has won international praise for its originality. The portions and presentation are of the nouvelle-cuisine variety, but the food is all organic. The wooden floors and crisp white tablecloths give the restaurant a classy feel that's in keeping with the standard of the food.

Skólabrú €€€€ *Skólabrú 1, tel: 562 4455.* Dining in this family house from the early 20th century makes you feel as if you could be eating in somebody's home. Real old-style service and beautifully presented food. The menu mixes Icelandic and international dishes, with an emphasis on seafood, duck and game.

Tveir Fiskar €€€€ *Geirsgata 9, tel: 511 3474.* If you want top quality and innovatively prepared fish for dinner, try this chi-chi restaurant situated down on the harbourside. It's owned by one of Iceland's top chefs, and the fish they serve here is of the very best quality, freshly landed and cooked to absolute perfection to ensure maximum customer satisfaction. Sadly, the prices are as imaginative as the cuisine.

Vegamót €€ *Vegamótastígur 4, tel: 511 3040.* Noisy, fashionable hang-out for Reykjavík's young crowd, where the staff can even text you their special offers. The menu is of the chicken, burgers and burritos variety, but the helpings are generous, and the atmosphere swings between hot and just plain warm. It's great for brunch, especially after a hard night's clubbing.

Verslunarfelagið Ida €€ *Lækjargata 2a, tel: 511 5001.* Sushi restaurant and cafe that is fast gaining a reputation for serving some of the best Japanese-style fish in Reykjavík. You'll also find a delicatessen store here selling Icelandic delicacies. Note that it's located on the first floor.

Þrír Frakkar €€ *Baldursgata 14, tel: 552 3939.* If you don't mind the plastic fish on the walls and the slightly chaotic feel of this little back-street French bistro, you will enjoy good food with generous helpings in a friendly atmosphere. Try the smoked puffin as a starter; the monkfish with vegetables and pesto is also delicious. If you're looking to try whale meat, this is the only restaurant in Reykjavík to feature it regularly on the menu. The restaurant is also renowned for its traditional dish of *þlokkfiskur* – a filling potato and fish mash which is always delicious.

EXCURSIONS

Blue Lagoon Restaurant €€€ *Blue Lagoon, Grindavík, tel: 426 8650.* Eat overlooking the thermal spa at this now world-famous spot. The menu uses fish brought ashore at the nearby harbour, but presents it in a variety of international dishes including bouillabaisse and curried cod. There are also chicken and pasta dishes, hamburgers and a children's menu. Best enjoyed after, rather than before, a dip in the hot waters.

Hótel Geysir €€ *Haukadal Biskupstungum, 801 Selfoss, tel: 486 8915.* This hotel's large dining room gets very busy with tour groups in summer. It offers an excellent, if unusual menu, including breast of guillemot and peking duck. The locally caught salmon is superb, as is the bread baked underground in the traditional Icelandic fashion. Good two- and three-course specials. Try to leave room for the sumptuous desserts.

INDEX